Understanding Utterances

Blackwell Textbooks in Linguistics

Understanding Utterances

Diane Blakemore

BLACKWELL
Oxford UK & Cambridge USA

First published 1992

Blackwell Publishers
108 Cowley Road
Oxford OX4 1JF
UK

Three Cambridge Center
Cambridge, Massachusetts 02142
USA

British Library Cataloguing in Publication Data

A CIP catalogue record for this book is available from
the British Library.

Library of Congress Cataloging-in-Publication Data

Blakemore, Diane.
   Understanding utterances/Diane Blakemore.
     p.   cm.—(Blackwell textbooks in linguistics: 6)
   Includes bibliographical references and index.
   ISBN 0–631–15866–9. — ISBN 0–631–15867–7 (pbk.)
   1. Pragmatics.   I. Title.   II. Series.
   P99.4.P72B5   1992
   306.4′4–dc20   91–44259
                                                              CIP

Typeset in 10 on 13 pt Sabon
by Tecset Ltd, Wallington
Printed in Great Britain by T.J. Press Ltd, Padstow

This book is printed on acid-free paper

For my daughter
Anna Louise
and
in memory of my grandmother
Anna Louisa Arcus

Contents

Preface

The question of what should be included in a book about pragmatics is surrounded by controversy. However, my aim in this book is not to trace the history of this controversy or to describe the various approaches that have been proposed, but rather to focus on one particular approach – the one taken by Sperber and Wilson in their Relevance Theory (Sperber and Wilson 1986). Here pragmatic interpretation is seen as a psychological matter, governed by a single cognitive principle, and the distinction between semantics and pragmatics is a psychological distinction based on the difference between linguistic and non-linguistic knowledge.

As a consequence, this book is both wider and narrower in scope than some readers might expect. It does include phenomena which will be recognized as central to virtually any book on pragmatics – for example, implicature, speech acts and the coherence of discourse. And it covers those phenomena which have raised problems for the relationship between semantics and pragmatics – for example, reference, presupposition and non-truth-conditional meaning. However, readers will not find any discussion of such things as the distribution of talk across participants in a conversation, the way in which conversations are opened or closed, or the means by which speakers and hearers attempt to save face. Moreover, it may be found that familiar pragmatic phenomena are discussed in less familiar terms. For example, the coherence of discourse is regarded not as evidence for the existence of a grammar of discourse, but as a result of the way in which hearers use contextual information in their search for relevance. And the fact that speakers may use language for purposes other than the description of states of affairs is not taken as evidence for the need for a social theory of speech acts, but is explained in terms of the different ways in which utterances may achieve relevance.

Readers will also find discussion of topics which are more usually found in books on literary theory than in books on pragmatics – in particular, metaphor, irony and other stylistic effects. The approach taken here will be familiar to some readers in that it does not see the interpretation of a literary text in terms of a system of rules and (culturally determined) codes. On the other hand, it differs from the Romantic approach to language (in both its old (see, for example, Shelley) and new (see, for example, Derrida) guises) in that it does not regard language as irremediably fuzzy.

The book is divided into three parts. The first serves as an introduction to the theoretical framework which is applied in the following two parts, and addresses such issues as the nature of communication, the definition and role of the context, the role of inference in utterance interpretation, and the dichotomy between semantic and pragmatic meaning. The second part deals with the recovery of the explicit content of utterances, and covers topics like reference assignment, the recovery of ellipsed material, the interpretation of non-declarative utterances, and the role of performative utterances. The final part is concerned with the recovery of implicit meaning and includes discussion of implicatures, the role of discourse connectives, and the interpretation of figurative utterances.

While my aim is not to present an overview of current pragmatic theories, I do try to indicate where and how Relevance Theory diverges from other approaches both in its general approach to communication and on specific issues. The notes play an important role here. I have also provided exercises and discussion topics in the text and at the end of sections to encourage readers to participate in the development of the framework, in its application in the analysis of the way utterances are understood, and in the debates between the competing theories.

Specific page references to Sperber and Wilson (1986) have not always been given in the text, but are supplied in the Recommended Reading lists at the end of each chapter. These lists are intended to provide reading suggestions for the main topics covered in each chapter. Further references are, of course, given in the text and notes, and sometimes accompany exercises.

I have referred to the speaker as *he* and the hearer as *she*. This decision has no intended contextual implications. I also use the term *speaker* to cover both speakers and writers, and the term *hearer* to cover both hearers and readers. Examples are numbered consecutively within each chapter.

Acknowledgements

This textbook is grounded in Dan Sperber and Deirdre Wilson's relevance-theoretic approach to communication and cognition, and I hope that it reflects at least some of the excitement I felt as a student during the development of their theory. I owe special thanks to Deirdre Wilson for her support and encouragement over the years and for her comments on early drafts on this book. Of course, it represents my interpretation of relevance theory, and any errors it may contain are my responsibility alone.

Bob Borsley and Robyn Carston have also given me a great deal of help and encouragement which is not always acknowledged in the text, and I would like to take the opportunity of thanking them here. As is the case with many textbooks, parts of this book have been tested out on unsuspecting students, and the finished product owes a great deal to the patience and enthusiasm of at least three generations of Linguistics students at Southampton University. Many thanks are due, too, to Jane Trask of Southampton for helping me produce a presentable manuscript and to the editorial team at Blackwell for their guidance and patience.

Finally, I wish to thank my family and friends for supporting and distracting me over the last three years.

The author and publisher are grateful to acknowledge permission to reprint copyright material as follows: To Spike Milligan Productions Ltd and the BBC for an extract from the *Goon Show Scripts*. To Gerald Duckworth and Penguin USA Inc., for an excerpt from Dorothy Parker's poem, 'Ninon de Lenclos on Her Last Birthday'. To Farrar, Straus & Giroux Inc., for Elizabeth Bishop's poem, 'Sleeping on the Ceiling'. I am also grateful to the Metropolitan Museum of Art for permission to reproduce the silver gelatin photograph, *Untitled*, by Jerry Uelsmann.

Part I   Fundamentals

1 Communication and the Context

1.1 What do Speakers Communicate?

It is difficult to think of many human activities that do not involve communication. We communicate with friends and with strangers, at work and at play, in public and in private. We communicate our knowledge and our ignorance, our anger and our pleasure, our needs and our intentions. Just as communication serves a variety of purposes it assumes a variety of forms. We may communicate by writing a book or making a speech, with a torrent of words or with one, with a grunt or with silence, by waving our arms or by raising our eyebrows. In some cases the means is chosen with great deliberation and care. In others the choice is spontaneous and virtually unconscious.

Given this diversity, the possibility of a theory of human communication might seem remote. Even if we confine ourselves, as we shall in this book, to the study of verbal communication, the task of encapsulating its nature and goals within a single principle or set of principles would seem to have very little chance of success. On the other hand, unless we are able to lay down the foundations for an integrated theory of communication, the observations that we make about our experiences of communication will remain just that – observations. There will be no systematic explanation of the fact that we may find one speaker witty and amusing, another long-winded and patronizing, that one style seems poetic while another seems prosaic, that one conversation seems coherent while another appears to go all over the place, that one remark seems puzzling while another seems trite and obvious.

But what sort of significance do such observations have? The problem is that different people are interested in communication for different reasons. For example, some writers are interested in communication for what it indicates about the structure of social interaction and the dynamics of social relationships. Accordingly, their accounts focus on such things as the distribution of talk across participants, the ways that conversations are opened and closed, the lengths that conversationalists go to in order to maintain agreement, and the means by which speakers and hearers attempt to save face.[1]

Other writers, however, are interested in communication for what it indicates about human psychology. That is, they proceed from the assumption that what is communicated is something that can be mentally represented – for example, a thought or desire – and they aim to characterize the mental processes by which the hearer discovers what is being communicated.

Now some writers, for example Stubbs (1983: 45–8), have criticized this psychological approach to communication on the grounds that it is restricted to the information or fact-giving role of language. Stubbs argues that it ignores not only the role of language in the expression of feelings, but also its many other functions. While we might characterize the examples in (1) in terms of the transmission of information, such a characterization would be misleading in the case of the examples in (2).

(1) (a) A: Can you tell me which buses go to the airport?
    B: A number ten or a number six.
  (b) The paper selector lever sets the type of paper feed the printer uses. It has two positions: forward and back. The front position is used with single sheet paper. The back position is used with continuous paper when the tractor-feed mechanism is installed.

(2) (a) A: Well, at least it isn't raining.
    B: No, not now anyway.
    A: Isn't it awful?
    B: Yes. I spent the whole weekend getting wet.
    A: I know. I spent the weekend drying shoes.
    B: They're all lined up on the radiators at our place.
    A: Yes, it's awful.
  (b) A: Why did the hedgehog cross the road?
    B: Why *did* the hedgehog cross the road?
    A: To visit his flat-mate.
  (c) A: I've failed. I know I've failed.
    B: Don't be stupid. Of course you haven't.
  (d) 'Tis not a year or two but show us a man,
    They are all but stomachs and we all but food;
    They eat us hungerly, and when they are full,
    They belch us.
                                        (*Othello*, III. iv)
  (e) Maggie, Maggie, Maggie,
    Out, out, out.
      (Chant often heard at political demonstrations during Mrs Thatcher's term of office as prime minister of Great Britain.)

These examples certainly demonstrate that communication has a social and an emotional dimension. However, this does not rule out the possibility of there being a psychological theory of communication any more than the fact that drinking alcohol has a social significance rules out the possibility of there being a physiological explanation for its effects on the liver. On the other hand, if we are to construct any kind of theory of communication at all, it must cover the kinds of examples in (2) as well as those in (1). And this means that communication cannot be construed simply as the transmission of information – at least not if by *information* is meant the representation of facts.[2] The answer to the question of what is communicated by a speaker must be more general than this.

The traditional answer to this question is that speakers communicate meanings. But then, the question becomes, what is a meaning? and, as readers will know, there is no generally accepted answer to this. For a start, it is clear that we need to distinguish between what the speaker means and what his words mean, or in other words, between *utterance meaning* and *sentence or word meaning*. What hearers are interested in, of course, is what the speaker means. Indeed, a hearer's interest in what the speaker means will often lead her to ignore the fact that his words mean something else. For example, in a television programme on holidays the presenter gave the following advice for those travelling in the Greek islands:

(3) Obviously, in the outer islands nobody speaks English. So brush up your English.

No viewer would have taken the presenter to be recommending that they improve their English for a holiday to Greece: the presenter could only have meant that they should brush up their Greek.

Similarly, hearers are usually able to discount the 'wrong' meaning(s) for ambiguous utterances and recover the meaning the speaker intended without making any conscious choice. For example, few travellers on the London Underground will have considered that (4) could be interpreted as restricting travel to those who carry dogs.

(4) Dogs must be carried.

As this example shows, it is not as if the hearer's knowledge of the meanings of the words used plays no role at all in the recovery of what the speaker means. The utterance in (4) could not, after all, be interpreted as an injunction to extinguish cigarettes. The hearer's knowledge of what the speaker's words mean only provides a clue as to what the speaker means, and she must build the speaker's meaning from this clue together with her knowledge of the context. In some cases, for instance (5) and (6), this clue is very skeletal indeed.

(5) Not in here.
(6) Telephone for you.

But, as we can see in (7), even when the speaker utters a complete sentence, there can be a variety of ways in which the meaning of his words falls short of what the hearer takes him to mean.

(7) There are too many marks in this book.

Is the speaker drawing attention to the kind of marks that would ruin the appearance of the book or the grades given to students after examinations? He has said there are too many of them. But too many for what? And what book is he referring to?

   Many philosophers and linguists would say that what the hearer builds from such linguistic clues is a *proposition* – that is, a representation of the state of affairs that she takes the hearer to be presenting as true. So, for example, in a situation in which a colleague is looking for the department secretary my utterance of (5) would be understood as expressing the proposition in (8).

(8) The department secretary is not in Diane Blakemore's office.[3]

However, it is generally recognized that what a speaker means on a particular occasion is not exhausted by the proposition he is taken to have expressed. The hearer is usually expected to derive other propositions which are not related in any systematic way to the meanings of the words uttered. Consider the following mini-dialogue:

(9) A: Is there any shopping to do?
      B: We'll be away for most of the weekend.

It is clear that B does not just mean that A and B will be away for most of the weekend. However, it is equally clear that what he means in addition to this cannot be regarded as part of the meaning of the words he utters. If, for example, the hearer holds the assumption in (10), then she will take B to be answering that there is no shopping to do. If, on the other hand, she holds the assumptions in (11), then she will take B to be implying that there is shopping to do.

(10) If we are going away for the weekend, then we won't need food.
(11) (a) If we are away for the weekend, then we won't be able to go shopping.
     (b) If we don't go shopping, then we won't have any food on our return.

This suggests that what the speaker means is a *set* of propositions, one of which is expressed directly through the meanings of the words he uses and the others conveyed indirectly and derived through inference. However, propositions are not just abstract entities to which assignments of truth and falsity are made. They are entertained in the mind as the objects of various attitudes – for example, belief, desire, certainty – and the same sentence can be used on different occasions to convey different attitudes towards the proposition it expresses. The problem with the psychological approach, according to some critics, is that it concerns itself only with those cases in which a proposition is presented as a true belief. If we are to meet this criticism, then we must account not only for the fact that beliefs are held with varying degrees of certainty, but also for the fact that propositions may be entertained as the objects of attitudes other than belief. For example, is the speaker of (12) simply asking the hearer to pretend that the proposition it expresses is true, or is he warning her that it is true?

(12) There's someone behind you.

Similarly, for a hearer to know what the speaker of (13) means she must know whether the utterance is an expression of dismay or relief, whether it is a prediction or a promise, a warning or a request for confirmation.

(13) Tom's coming.

In these examples the linguistic form of the utterance is of very little help to the hearer in the identification of the speaker's attitude. However, the gap between the sentence meaning and the utterance meaning may be narrowed by the use of lexical or syntactic means. For example:

(14) (a) Suppose that there is someone behind you.
     (b) I warn you that there is someone behind you.
(15) (a) I promise that Tom is coming.
     (b) Is Tom coming?

This suggests that whenever a speaker communicates he must make a decision as to what he chooses to make explicit and what he chooses to leave implicit. It is not as if (15a) communicates something different from (13), interpreted in the appropriate context. Rather they differ in the amount of help the hearer is given in recovering whatever is communicated. In other words, they differ in *style*. But what determines the speaker's choice of style?

Some writers (for example, Leech (1983)) have concentrated on the sociological and cultural factors governing the form of a speaker's message. So, for example, the speaker's decision to produce the utterance in (16) rather than the one in (17) may be said to be governed by social conventions concerning verbosity.

(16)   I had two pieces of toast and a cup of coffee for breakfast.
(17)   Breakfast is the first meal of the day. I had two slices of bread toasted under a flame until crisp and spread with butter and a sweet confection known as jam. I also had a cup of a hot beverage made from roasted and ground beans of a plant grown in South America and Africa infused in hot water.

And in (18) speaker B's decision to give an indirect rather than direct answer may be said to be governed by cultural norms concerning politeness or tact.

(18)   A: Come and have a drink this evening.
       B: I'm afraid I have to go to a meeting.

I am not suggesting that cultural and social factors do not govern the form of utterances or that these factors are not worthy of study.[4] However, it is not clear that such a study could account for all forms of stylistic variation or for the relationship between context and linguistic meaning in utterance interpretation. For example, what socio-cultural factors would explain the speaker's decision to give the indirect answer in (19) rather than the direct one in (20)?

(19)   A: Do you like rugby?
       B: I *am* a New Zealander.
(20)   A: Do you like rugby?
       B: Yes I do.

The difference between these two answers lies in the way that they are processed, and, in particular, in that the interpretation of the indirect answer depends on the hearer's ability to supply the contextual information that all New Zealanders are rugby fans. (I do not, of course, subscribe to this belief.) That is, by answering indirectly, the speaker encourages the hearer to speculate on – perhaps draw conclusions from – a piece of information which she would not have derived from the direct answer. More generally, in order to understand such stylistic effects as verbosity, pomposity, obscurity and terseness we need to have some understanding of the processes involved in the recovery of what is communicated.

So far we have restricted the discussion to examples in which the form of the speaker's utterance contributes not to what is communicated, but to the way in which the hearer is guided in the recovery of what is communicated. In other words, in these examples we can maintain a distinction between content (what is communicated) and style (how it is communicated). However, there are examples of stylistic variation in which this distinction is more difficult to maintain. Recall Emilia's utterance in (2d) (repeated here).

(2d)   'Tis not a year or two but show us a man,
         They are all but stomachs and we all but food;
         They eat us hungerly, and when they are full,
         They belch us.

Obviously, Emilia does not mean that men are stomachs and women food. At least not literally. But then what does she mean? Perhaps (21) conveys the gist of what she means.

(21)   Women are exploited by men.

But if she meant this, why did she say what she said? For effect, you might say. But what is this effect? If it is not part of what Emilia communicated, then (21) would be an adequate paraphrase of (2d). And of course it is not. Emilia did not just mean that women are exploited by men. The problem is that it is impossible to spell out what she meant without distortion or loss of meaning. There is no single proposition that Emilia meant.

It might be objected here that this is hardly an ordinary example of communication and that it should be dealt with by a theory of literary meaning rather than a theory of the way ordinary people understand utterances. And, indeed, until recently, the only writers who have been concerned with these aspects of communication have been literary theorists.[5] I would not wish to suggest that there are no aspects of literary meaning which are not beyond the scope of the kind of theory we are trying to develop here. On the other hand, it seems that there are perfectly ordinary examples of communication that present the same kind of problem. I do not have in mind here just the mundane, non-literary examples of figurative language found in ordinary communication, but there are non-figurative examples of communication in which it is not possible to pin down exactly what the speaker meant. Consider, for example, the mini-dialogue in (22):

(22)   A: What shall we do this evening?
       B: I'm really tired.

Obviously, B is intending to convey something more than the information that
he is really tired. But what? That he doesn't want to do anything? That he
doesn't want to do anything energetic? That he can't be bothered thinking
about it? Although the hearer isn't expected to derive just any conclusion from
B's response, it seems that there is no one single conclusion that she is expected
to derive.

Sometimes the speaker's intentions are even more vague than this. Think of
when you draw someone's attention to a view or a piece of music by producing
some sort of appreciative noise or gesture. Your companion knows she must
attend to something good. But what? The point is, of course, that there is no
need for her to assume that you meant her to notice anything in particular.
Moreover, there is no need for her to think that you could have expressed your
thought about what you are seeing/hearing more precisely.

Notice that the problem here is not that you are not Shakespeare. Perhaps
Shakespeare would have done a better job of describing what he had seen. But
this is not because his description could have enabled the reader to paraphrase
his meaning in a single description. On the contrary, it is because it would have
evoked a whole range of thoughts and impressions. But what is an impression?
It is easy to see why anyone wanting to give a precise account of verbal
communication would be tempted to avoid these sorts of examples and focus
on the ones where the speaker's meaning can be spelled out. Not only is it hard
to say what an impression is, but also it is not clear what, if anything, we can
say about the mental processes involved in recovering one. However, in
succumbing to this temptation we would be leaving ourselves open to the
charge of excessive narrowness made by Stubbs. The challenge, then, is to give
a precise account of something that is very imprecise. More particularly, it is to
give an account of the processes involved in interpreting utterances produced
by speakers whose intentions range from the very specific to the very vague.

1.2   Understanding and Inference

Utterance interpretation takes place so fast and so spontaneously that we are
usually not aware of how we recover the message we do. Fortunately, we are
not often called upon to justify the interpretation we give to an utterance.

Nevertheless let us see whether we can view ourselves in slow motion as we tackle the following examples.

First, the example of the slip of the tongue mentioned above which is repeated here as (23). Remember that the speaker is a presenter of a travel programme giving advice for travellers in the Greek islands.

(23) Obviously, in the outer islands nobody speaks English. So brush up your English.

Why would a viewer interpret this as an injunction to improve her Greek? It is likely that she would have reasoned along the following lines:

> If nobody speaks English in this place, then English travellers would have to speak the native language which is Greek. Since most English travellers do not know Greek, this means that they would have to learn it. So the presenter must have meant 'Brush up your Greek'.

Next, an example of an ambiguous utterance heard in a news item about the restoration of a church:

(24) The cushions will be replaced by volunteers.

The 'other' interpretation for this is so unlikely that you will be forgiven for taking a while to recover it. Why do we not assume that the news reader meant that the volunteers will be used instead of cushions? Because he was talking about how the fabric of the church was to be replaced, because cushions are used for sitting (or kneeling) on, and people don't go around sitting on other people.

Finally, a dialogue which will be familiar to many readers:

(25) A: What's on television?
B: (*consulting the newspaper*) Nothing.

Does B mean literally nothing? Since the television stations are not on strike and tonight is like any other – the government hasn't banned television on Tuesdays – A will assume that B really meant 'Nothing worth watching'.

Three important points emerge from this very intuitive discussion:

1 In each case the explanation for the interpretation recovered has the appearance of a (very informally presented and often truncated) logical

argument. In other words, the hearer uses reasoning or inference in recovering what is communicated.

2 In each case the inferences the hearer makes depend on contextual information – that is, information which is not derived from the meanings of the words uttered but from her knowledge of the world.

3 In each case the inferences the hearer makes appeal to the assumption that the speaker has met or has tried to meet certain standards.

If we want a less intuitive explanation of the way people understand utterances, then we will have to address the following questions, which arise from these points:

1 What is the nature of the inferential computations that are involved in utterance interpretation?

2 What is the source of contextual assumptions used in the interpretation process and how are they selected?

3 What exactly are the standards that communicators aim to meet and what is their origin – for example, are they fundamentally cultural or social norms, or do they have their source in human psychology?

This section is concerned with the first question.

In an introductory logic book *inference* means *deduction* and would be introduced by means of examples like (26).

(26) All men are mortal.   (premise)
      Socrates is a man.   (premise)
      _____

      Socrates is mortal.   (conclusion)

(27) He drank either the water or the milk.   (premise)
      He didn't drink the water.   (premise)
      _____

      He drank the milk.   (conclusion)

What place do such inferences have in the interpretation of utterances in ordinary discourse? None, say some authors – or at least very little.

> It may be the case that we are capable of deriving a specific conclusion . . . from specific premises . . . via deductive inference, but we are rarely asked to do so in the everyday discourse we encounter . . . We are

more likely to operate with a rather loose form of inferencing. (G. Brown and Yule 1983: 33–4[6])

According to Brown and Yule, this looseness derives from the fact that the inferences made in everyday discourse are only *likely* to be right, and that in another context they might be abandoned. Recall, for example, the interpretation given for (25) (repeated here).

(25)   A: What's on television?
       B: Nothing.

On the assumption that everything is as normal and the television workers are not on strike, the hearer would take B to mean 'Nothing worth watching'. But of course, he *could* have continued as in (28).

(28)   Nothing. All the TV stations are on strike.

Similarly, a hearer can only assume that the conclusion she derives from B's utterance in (29) on the basis of the assumption in (30) is probably right, because in another context (think of one for yourself) she may draw an entirely different conclusion.

(29)   A: Are you going to the seminar?
       B: It's on pragmatics.
(30)   B goes to anything that is on pragmatics.

Indeed, there is no limit to the premises that the hearer *could* supply. Here's a possible context that you probably didn't think of:

(31)   If the seminar is on pragmatics, very few people will attend.
       If very few people attend the seminar, then I won't be able to hide my knitting.
       I can knit only if I can hide it.

In certain kinds of jokes speakers exploit the way in which inferences may be cancelled for humorous effect.

(32)   A very agitated lady got her doctor on the phone. 'Come quick', she cried, 'My son has just swallowed a fountain pen'. The doctor remained calm. 'I'll be over as soon as I can', he said, 'but there are several patients in the waiting room. You may not see me for three or four hours'. 'Three

or four hours' echoed the lady, 'What shall I do in the meantime?'
'You'll just have to use a pencil', said the doctor. (Bennet A. Cerf,
Laughing Stock)

In contrast, a deductive inference is valid in all contexts. There is no further
information that could render either of the inferences in (26) and (27) invalid.

Does this mean, as Levinson (1983: 114–16), for example, suggests it does,
that the inferences hearers make in the course of utterance interpretation are
probabilistic or inductive? That would be unfortunate, because as Fodor
(1983) points out, while the psychology of deductive inferences has been very
well studied, relatively little is known about the psychology of inductive
systems.

But the fact that the hearer of an utterance could in principle have brought
different assumptions to bear on its interpretation does not mean that the
inferences she actually does make are inductive. Obviously, different sets of
premises may be supplied by different hearers on different occasions.
However, on each occasion the hearer performs a deductive inference from a
specific set of premises. Moreover, although it is logically possible that the
hearer could bring any assumptions to bear on the interpretation of a given
utterance, this is clearly not psychologically possible. Is it really plausible that
speaker B in (29) could have intended the hearer to supply the premises in
(31)? It is evident that the hearer's choice of context, and hence her
interpretation, is constrained by her assumption that the speaker is answering
the question. More generally, she is constrained by her assumption that the
utterance conforms to certain general standards. On the other hand, since
interpretation varies from individual to individual, there is no point in trying to
devise a rule or algorithm for computing the correct set of premises (and hence
the correct interpretation). As you will have experienced, hearers' choice of
contextual premises does not always match the ones envisaged by the speaker.
People do get their wires crossed.

This is not the place for a detailed examination of the inference systems that
are (or may be) involved in the interpretation of utterances.[7] However, there is
one important point to be made before we go on to discuss the selection of
contextual premises. A logician's interest in deductive inference lies in the fact
that it is *truth-preserving*. To say that an inference is valid is to say that the
truth of the premises guarantees the truth of the conclusion. It doesn't matter
whether the premises are in fact true. If the inference is valid, then it is
impossible for the premises to be true and the conclusion false. Here, however,
we are interested in inference rules as they apply to propositions which are
stored as factual descriptions of the world – that is, to assumptions. And
assumptions are not just either true or false. They are held with varying degrees
of strength depending on the way they are acquired. For example, assumptions

derived through direct observation are held with very strong conviction, while the strength of an assumption derived as the result of the interpretation of an utterance depends on the degree of confidence the hearer has in the speaker.

Exercise 1

Consider how the strength of your conviction in the following assumption varies in each of the situations (a) to (e).

Barbara plays the violin.
 (a)   You see Barbara carrying a violin case.
 (b)   Somebody tells you that Barbara cannot play the violin.
 (c)   You hear the strains of a violin coming from Barbara's house.
 (d)   You see (and hear) Barbara playing a violin.
 (e)   Barbara tells you that she cannot play the violin.

As you will recognize from the above exercise, the strength of an assumption may be affected by new evidence. For example, your assumption derived on the basis of (a) will be strengthened by your experience described in (d). In contrast, supposing that you have faith in Barbara's own word, (e) gives you stronger evidence for the falsity of the assumption than (a) does for its truth, and consequently Barbara's utterance will lead you to reject the assumption that you derived on the basis of (a).

As we shall see, the desire to improve the strength of our existing assumptions plays a central part in the way we interpret utterances. My point here, though, is simply that the inference system we use in utterance interpretation must be geared to this fact. That is, the inferences must be such that the conclusion inherits its strength from the strength of the premises. More specifically, the conclusion can only be as strong as the weakest premise. Let me demonstrate this point by returning to the exercise above. I assume that you derive the assumption that Barbara plays the violin from your observation in (a) by means of a deduction something along the lines of (33).

(33)   If someone carries a violin case, then they play the violin.   (premise)
       Barbara is carrying a violin case.   (premise)
       _____

       Barbara plays the violin.   (conclusion)

Obviously, the second premise is very strong since it is derived from direct perceptual evidence. But the first premise is not as strong (there could be a gun in the case), and consequently the conclusion can only be as strong as this premise.

1.3 The Context

It is easy enough to see how you might obtain the second premise in the above deduction. This is immediately accessible information derived through your perceptual system. But what about the first one? This is not so immediately accessible and has to be derived from your memory. But how? And in what format is it stored?

Let us see how these questions arise in the case of utterance interpretation.

As is frequently pointed out, the hearer in a discourse has immediate access to information made available through the interpretation of the preceding text. For example, given the interpretation of the first utterance in the sequence in (34), the second will be interpreted as (35).

(34) (*I am on the telephone in Southampton talking to a friend in Kent*)
        It's raining over here. Do you still want to come?
(35) In view of the fact that it is raining in Southampton do you want to come here (to Southampton) as you had planned?

Of course, not all utterances are part of a text (or discourse). This is not to say, however, that the hearer does not necessarily have direct access to contextual information. In the following example, the hearer uses information derived from observation in order to recover the interpretation in (37).

(36) (*It suddenly starts raining*)
        What shall we do now?
(37) What shall we do now that it is raining?

However, in many cases the information that the hearer has immediately accessible either from direct observation or from the interpretation of the immediately preceding discourse is not sufficient to enable her to understand the speaker's utterance. Consider, for example, the following dialogue, which was part of a conversation about my holiday in Wales.

(38) COLLEAGUE: The place I've always wanted to visit is . . . what's it called . . . Portmeirion.
        ME: Oh yes. We went there. It's really strange.

COLLEAGUE: Is it?

ME: Yes. And full of tourists. Really crowded. Anyway, I went to Number Six's house.

I suspect that many readers will be as baffled as my colleague by my last contribution. I had mistakenly assumed that he knew that Portmeirion was the setting for a cult television series called 'The Prisoner', in which the hero was referred to as Number Six. More accurately, I had assumed that the mention of Portmeirion would have given him access to this information which he had stored in memory. In other words, I had assumed that he could extend his *initial context* provided by the interpretation of the immediately preceding discourse by accessing information stored in memory under an entry *Portmeirion*.

As I have said, I was mistaken and communication failed at this point. We'll be discussing this shortly. Meanwhile let us see what this example shows about the structure of our memories and the way that information is accessed from memory for use in the interpretation of utterances.

The fundamental idea is that contextual information is stored under a *concept* or *address* (for example, *Portmeirion*), and that the hearer is given access to this address (and the information stored under it) when the concept is presented to him for processing (for example, in discourse). In other words, we are assuming that information has constituents – concepts – and that the presentation of a concept gives the hearer access to further information, which itself is made up of concepts which give her access to still further information, and so on.

In this example, the information which I had assumed the hearer would access was idiosyncratic: information about a particular place. But as many writers have pointed out, there is a case for assuming that people have stereotypical assumptions about frequently encountered objects or events.[8] To take a variation on a well-worn example, the interpretation of the sequence in (39) depends on the hearer's stereotypical knowledge that waiters work in restaurants and that restaurants serve food.

(39) Tom was hungry. He told the waiter to bring him two large steaks and a large portion of vegetables.

Such knowledge, it is claimed, is not stored as individual assumptions, but as part of a chunk – sometimes called a frame or schema – which is accessed as a whole. Thus in the above example the required contextual information could be part of a restaurant frame.

However, as G. Brown and Yule (1983: 240) point out, not all the information in a frame is relevant for the interpretation of a particular utterance. For example, a restaurant frame might include not only information about waiters, but also information about the people who prepare and cook the food, the furniture, menus and the cost of meals, etc. This leaves us with the question of how hearers select from their total knowledge chunk the particular information that they bring to bear in the interpretation process. Moreover, since a text or discourse can in principle give the hearer access to a number of different knowledge chunks – for example, the hearer of (39) might be given access not only to a restaurant frame but also a vegetable frame – it must be explained why not all of these are actually used in the interpretation of a particular utterance.

This is really a version of the question posed earlier – how does the hearer select the context for the interpretation of an utterance? – and it will arise as long as we continue to adopt a psychological view of the context. That is, it will arise as long as we continue to think of the context in terms of assumptions or beliefs held by the hearer. A hearer has in principle access to an enormous amount of background information, and in principle any of this could be used in the interpretation of an utterance. But hearers do not interpret utterances in just any context. As we have seen, successful communication depends on the hearer selecting the *right* assumptions – the ones that yield the intended interpretation. How does this occur?

It is important to stress here that we are not restricting the context either to the immediate physical environment or to the immediately preceding text or discourse. As I have said, we are defining it in psychological terms as a subset of the hearer's beliefs and assumptions about the world.[9] These may be derived from such sources. But we have also seen that the interpretation of an utterance may depend on the hearer's ability to supply certain assumptions from memory. These range from strongly evidenced assumptions derived through perception to guesses and hypotheses. They include memories of particular occasions and about particular individuals, general cultural assumptions, religious beliefs, knowledge of scientific laws, assumptions about the speaker's emotional state and assumptions about other speakers' perception of your emotional state.

Given this conception of the context, you might wonder how successful communication is ever possible. For, surely, communication can succeed only if the context that the hearer brings to bear is identical to the one envisaged by the speaker, and the contents of people's memories are highly idiosyncratic. Obviously, the members of the same society or cultural group share a common framework of beliefs and assumptions. However, there are always differences which lead not only to difference in the events memorized, but also to different interpretations of the same events.

In fact, according to one approach, the requirement that the context consist of shared assumptions is not strong enough. Consider the following artificial example (which is a variation on an example given by H. Clark and Marshall (1981: 11–12)):

(40)   My colleague R and I sometimes meet for morning coffee and lately we have been discussing a committee meeting which we are both meant to attend on Friday. On Thursday I go to coffee via the post-room and find amongst my mail a notice that this meeting is to be cancelled in favour of an emergency meeting of the whole faculty. No mention of this is made during coffee, but as we leave R says:
I'll see you at the meeting then.

Which meeting is R referring to? Since we have discussed the committee meeting on various occasions, I know that R knows this meeting is taking place and that I know it's taking place. But he might think that I have picked up my mail and on this basis be referring to the meeting of the whole faculty. On the other hand, he might think that although I have picked up my mail I have no way of knowing that he has and so will be referring to the committee meeting. Or, he might have seen the notice and think that I know that he has seen it but does not know that I know that he knows I know that he has seen it.

And so on. The suggestion is that the only way to guarantee successful communication is for me not only to know that there is a meeting of the faculty on Friday, but also to know that R knows about this meeting, and to know that R knows that I know about it, and that R knows that I know that he knows about it and so on. In other words, the only way to guarantee successful communication is for R and me to have what Schiffer (1972) called *mutual knowledge*.[10]

When I introduced the example I warned you that it was artificial. Ordinary communication just isn't like this. For a start, whereas utterance interpretation takes place over a finite – and often a very short – time, utterance interpretation that depends on the speaker and hearer establishing mutual knowledge must take an indefinite time. H. Clark and Marshall (1981: 24–33) argue that this problem is only apparent since there is a finite inductive procedure for identifying mutual knowledge. They claim that a speaker and hearer can assume mutual knowledge of a proposition in virtue of their joint presence in a situation which supplies evidence for its truth. Obviously, the strength of this evidence may vary. For example, they claim that physical co-presence provides the strongest evidence for mutual knowledge since the participants need only make minimal further assumptions to justify their conclusion. If, for example, we are sitting outside and a plane flies very low overhead, then we need only assume that each other is rational and has normal perceptual abilities in order to justify the conclusion that we have mutual knowledge of the plane. Linguistic co-presence provides less direct evidence: two people presented with the same utterance may conclude that they have mutual knowledge of the proposition it expresses only if they also assume that the expressions used belong to a language they both know and that the utterance was not part of a code or some other non-standard use of language. Finally, community membership may provide evidence for mutual knowledge in the sense that if speaker and hearer can establish that they belong to the same community, then, given certain other assumptions, they can assume mutual knowledge of all the propositions known by its members.

These proposals seems to assume that all knowledge is based on the evidence of observable data. However, to acquire knowledge of a physical object or event is to derive a mental representation – a particular description – of it, and while the existence of a physical object might be self-evident to a person with normal perceptual abilities, many auxiliary assumptions are needed before she can establish knowledge of it under a particular description. Because these auxiliary assumptions are not necessarily themselves part of the available observable data, but are supplied from memory, two people may derive two different representations of the same object or event. This suggests that a speaker and hearer can guarantee that they have mutual knowledge only if they have access to the contents of each other's memory. Obviously, the fact that it is impossible for anyone to have access to anyone else's memory does not prevent successful communication from taking place.

One possible counter-argument here might be that while speakers and hearers cannot be expected to establish complete mutual knowledge, they do try to establish it to a certain degree. But to what degree? Just how much work are speakers and hearers prepared to do to avoid misunderstanding?

It is here that we come to the second respect in which our example was artificial. Obviously, communication does require co-ordination between speaker and hearer in that misunderstandings occur when there is a mismatch between the context envisaged by the speaker and the one selected by the hearer. But this is not to say that speakers and hearers do not proceed until they can guarantee that communication will succeed. The successes in every-day communication suggest that speakers and hearers do not aim to establish mutual knowledge before they proceed, but make all sorts of assumptions and guesses. As we have seen in the example in (38), these assumptions may be mistaken. Communication does sometimes fail. But in the event of a misunderstanding you do not find the speaker and hearer wishing that they had devoted more time to establishing mutual knowledge or resolving that they will take greater care in establishing mutual knowledge in the future. No matter how much work a speaker and hearer might be prepared to do in order to establish mutual knowledge, this will not be enough to ensure that the intended interpretation of the utterance will be recovered. In interpreting the utterance in (41) the hearer will aim to select a context which supplies a specific referent for the definite description *the book*.

(41) The book is in the library.

But presumably both speaker and hearer have mutual knowledge of several if not dozens of books. In other words, the mutual knowledge framework can only define a class of possible contexts and cannot explain how the actual context and hence the actual interpretation is identified.

As I have said, communication is a risky business. There is no fail-safe way of ensuring that the book that the hearer takes the speaker to mean is in fact the one he intended to mean. However, if the speaker's attempt to communicate was genuine, then he must have assumed (correctly or incorrectly) that the hearer could access the right context. Otherwise what would have been the point of speaking in the first place?

According to the discussion so far, assuming that the hearer can access the right context means assuming that the required contextual assumptions are already available to her. However, consider the following example (taken from Sperber and Wilson (1986)): Suppose Mary and Peter are looking at a landscape where Mary has noticed a distant church. She says to him:

(42) I've been inside that church.

As Sperber and Wilson go on to say, Mary doesn't stop to ask herself whether Peter has noticed that the building is a church or even whether he has noticed the building at all. Certainly, she doesn't ask herself whether he has noticed that she has noticed or whether he has noticed that she has noticed that he has noticed. 'All she has is reasonable confidence that he will be able to identify the building as a church when required to' (1986: 43). In fact, it might have been only on the strength of Mary's utterance that it becomes evident to him that the building is a church. He might have thought that it was a castle. That is, shared knowledge is a result of, rather than a prerequisite for, successful communication. The only prerequisite is that Peter is able to supply certain assumptions at the appropriate moment.

Everyday conversation is full of such examples. Let us look at just one more. Suppose that Mary has asked Peter whether he has read a certain book. Peter suspects that Mary does not know that this book has won a literary prize. Even so, he may expect her to conclude from his utterance in (43) that he has not read the book.

(43) I never read books that win prizes.

Clearly, the information that Mary needs in order to derive this conclusion is not part of their shared knowledge before Peter produces the utterance. Peter expects that Mary will be able to supply this information as part of the interpretation of the utterance. In other words, he assumes not that Mary will have the right context in advance of the utterance, but that she will construct it in the course of interpreting the utterance.

In both these examples the speaker takes a risk. However, even at an intuitive level we can see that it is a risk worth taking. In the next chapter we shall see why.

Recommended Reading

Communication and Pragmatics (Sperber and Wilson)

Sperber and Wilson 1986: 3–15 (critique of semiotic approach to communication), 24–31 (discussion of Grice's approach).
Leech 1983: 1–17 (a socio-cultural approach to pragmatics).

A History of the Term Pragmatics

Levinson 1983: 1–5.

The Context

Sperber and Wilson 1986: 15–21, 38–46; 1982 (a critique of the mutual-knowledge approach).
Leech 1983: 13–15 (a socio-cultural approach).
G. Brown and Yule 1983 (a discussion of the context in discourse analysis).
H. Clark and Marshall 1981 (mutual knowledge).
Bach and Harnish 1979: 4–6 (an approach based on mutual knowledge).
Lewis 1972, 1979 (a formal semantics approach).

Inference

Sperber and Wilson 1986: ch. 2.
Levinson 1983: 113–16.
G. Brown and Yule 1983: 33–5.

Notes

1   For examples of this approach see P. Brown and Levinson (1979), Owen (1983) and Sacks, Schegloff and Jefferson (1974).

2 cf. Dretske (1981).
3 For want of a better medium I have to represent propositions in a natural language – in this case, English.
4 See, for example, the work on honorifics in Levinson (1979) and that on politeness and social markers by P. Brown and Levinson (1978, 1979).
5 See section 3.2 for further discussion.
6 See also Levinson (1983: 114–15).
7 See Sperber and Wilson (1986), chapter 2, for further discussion.
8 See G. Brown and Yule (1983: 236–56) for an introduction to these notions.
9 Defining the context in psychological terms makes it a unitary concept. That is, in contrast with a number of authors (for example, Allan 1986, Leech 1983), we do not distinguish between discourse context, social context and physical context.
10 Lewis (1969) calls it common knowledge.

2 Relevance

2.1 Standards in Communication

I don't know how many readers will find the following extract funny – I suspect that it loses something in the translation from radio to the printed page. However, funny or not, it is certainly peculiar, and it is worth considering why.

PETER: When the Englishman awoke he found himself in a tall dark room with sideboards – it was a prison cell.
SEAGOON: True, true. The only other occupant was another occupant – apart from that he was the *only* other occupant. He was chained to the wall by a chain which was attached to the wall – he *appeared* to be a man of breeding and intellect.
ECCLES: Hello dere.
SEAGOON: I was wrong. (But could he be Fred Nurke?)
ECCLES: How's your old dad, eh?
SEAGOON: Do you recognize this banana?
ECCLES: Nope – I don't think I've ever met him before.
SEAGOON: Then are you one banana short?
ECCLES: Nope, I ain't one short.
SEAGOON: Aha, then you're not Fred Nurke.
ECCLES: Ohh, ain't I?
SEAGOON: No.
ECCLES: You mean I'm somebody else?
SEAGOON: Yes.

. . .

SEAGOON: Is there any other way out of here?
ECCLES: Would you like to share my supper?
SEAGOON: Ahh, how about that window there?
ECCLES: Oh, you can't eat that.

(Spike Milligan, *The Goon Show Scripts*)

The effect may be comic, but the point it illustrates is quite serious. The participants in this dialogue simply don't behave like normal rational speakers and hearers. In fact, it is not clear whether they are genuinely trying to communicate at all. The following exercise contains a real-life example which underlines this point.

Exercise 1

Mr X had suffered a stroke leaving him paralysed on one side and making speech difficult. However, his actual capacity for language was unimpaired – for example, he was not aphasic. Mrs X visited him in hospital every other day. It was Monday and as she left she said, 'Well, see you Tuesday then.' Mr X's (rather difficult to decipher) reply was, 'What day is it?' Mrs X immediately panicked and drew the conclusion that the stroke had affected Mr X's mental faculties after all.[1]

Why is Mrs X's reaction unjustified and what is the moral?

As these examples show, a speaker will not be assumed to be communicating unless he is assumed to be rational, or in other words, unless he is thought to be conforming to certain norms or standards. As an exercise, you might like to formulate the norms suggested by the examples we have considered. It is likely that this will raise a number of questions – for example, what is it to be genuinely informative? when is a discourse coherent? what are the procedures by which a hearer judges a speaker's contribution to be in accordance with his existing assumptions? However, the most fundamental question of all (at least for a psychological approach to utterance interpretation) is: assuming such norms have their basis in human rationality, how are we to derive them from the goals of human communication? And that, of course, presupposes that we know what these norms are.

The idea that communication is governed by norms which have their basis in human rationality is due to the philosopher H. P. Grice (1975, 1989).[2]

> Our talk exchanges . . . are characteristically, to some degree at least, co-operative efforts; and each participant recognises in them, to some extent, a common purpose or set of purposes, or at least a mutually accepted direction . . . We might then formulate a rough general principle which participants will be expected (ceteris paribus) to observe, namely: Make your conversational contribution such as required, at the stage at which it occurs, by the accepted purpose or direction of the talk exchange in which you are engaged. (Grice 1989: 26)

Grice develops this principle, which he calls the Co-operative Principle, into a number of maxims:

Maxims of Quantity
   1   Make your contribution as informative as required.
   2   Do not make your contribution more informative than is required.
Maxims of Quality
   1   Do not say what you believe to be false.
   2   Do not say that for which you lack adequate evidence.
Maxim of Relation
Be relevant.
Maxims of Manner
   1   Avoid obscurity of expression.
   2   Avoid ambiguity.
   3   Be brief.
   4   Be orderly.

Grice's main concern was with the role of these maxims in the explanation of the way speakers may communicate more than what they actually say. However, many so-called Gricean accounts of utterance interpretation do not recognize that Grice's account leaves many basic questions unanswered. Indeed, in the absence of answers to these questions it is sometimes difficult to say what constitutes a genuine Gricean explanation. Here, however, we are not so much concerned with the question of what Grice really meant as with the questions raised by his approach, in particular, with a general question Grice himself asked: is it possible to find a basis for the maxims? If it isn't and they simply describe how people happen to behave, then it is difficult to see how they could provide the basis for an explanatory theory of utterance interpretation. But what kind of explanatory theory do we want? If we say, as for example Leech (1983: 10) has, that the maxims have their origin in the nature of society or culture, then we will have a socio-cultural theory of communication which will vary from society to society or from culture to culture. Obviously, we do need an account of the way in which socio-cultural factors affect interpretation. However, this is not necessarily to say that variation in interpretation is a consequence of variation in the norms governing communication, and that there cannot be a universal theory of utterance interpretation which is based in human cognition.

It seems that although Grice regarded a social account of the maxims as a possibility, he concluded that such a theory would not have the requisite universality:

I would like to be able to show that observance of the Co-operative Principle and maxims is reasonable (rational) along the following lines: that anyone who cares about the goals which are central to communica-tion . . . must be expected to have an interest, given suitable circum-stances, in participation in talk exchanges which will be profitable only on the assumption that they will be conducted in general accordance with the C[o-operative] P[rinciple] and the maxims. (Grice 1989: 29–30)

However, he also warns us that the key to such an explanation lies in the notion of relevance, a notion which his account leaves undefined.

Sperber and Wilson's Relevance Theory could be regarded as an attempt to develop Grice's basic insight. They argue that the key to an explanation of human communication lies in the notion of relevance, a notion which is grounded in a general view of human cognition. As they point out, they are not attempting to define the ordinary English word *relevance*. Their aim is to characterize a property of mental processes which the ordinary notion of *relevance* approximates. That is, their notion of relevance is a technical one. However, as a prelude to the more technical discussion which follows you could attempt the following exercise. This should enable you to identify two very important properties of relevance (in the sense being developed here).

Exercise 2

1   What would be your reaction if I were to tell you at the end of this section that:

(a)   my brother lives in New Zealand?
(b)   you are now reading a book about utterance interpretation?
(c)   the next section is about the principle of relevance?
(d)   the rest of this book will be written in Maori?

2   Discuss the difference between uttering the sentence below (a) in a conversation during lunch, and (b) in a conversation with an official from the television-licensing authority:

I haven't got a television.

Now, join me in a bit of make-believe. Suppose that you have an appointment with me in my office, but that I am on the phone when you arrive. There are all sorts of things that you *could* notice as you wait – the smell of coffee, the clock on the window-sill, the murmur of voices in the next room, my Antipodean accent, the pile of German books on my desk, an open desk diary with your name scrawled on the page and so on. And on the basis of this evidence there are all sorts of assumptions that you *could* form – that I've just had a cup of coffee, that there are people in the next room, that I'm not English, that I understand German, that I was expecting to see you and so on. Following Sperber and Wilson, let us call the set of assumptions that you could form your *cognitive environment*.

Now, obviously you cannot attend to everything – even in this limited space. And obviously, you do not form just any assumptions on the basis of what you do attend to. The question is, what makes you attend to some things rather than others, and why do you make certain assumptions rather than others? In some cases it is as if you have no choice. Anyone would be much more likely to attend to the ringing of a telephone than the ticking of a clock. And given that they do notice the telephone ringing, anyone would be much more likely to form the assumption that someone is phoning me than the assumption that my telephone works. Other cases, though, may be less standard. Why is it, for example, that you attend to the fact that my clock says 4.45 or that there is a pile of German books on my desk?

Now, suppose that you have arrived at my office in order to carry out a questionnaire on computing and word-processing needs, and that you haven't been able to find out what department I am in. According to the directory in the foyer, there are two departments on this floor: German and Philosophy. On the basis of this, you form the disjunctive assumption in (1).

(1)   DB is in either the German department or the Philosophy department.

Let us suppose further that you hold the assumption in (2).

(2)   If DB is in the German department, then she will want a printer with a German character set.

Of course, you intend to ask me what department I'm in, but as you wait you look around for clues – for example, the pile of German books on my desk. Combined with the assumption in (3) the existence of these books allows you to derive the assumption in (4), which combined with the earlier assumption in (2) will allow you to derive the conclusion in (5).

(3)   If someone has German books on their desk, then they are a member of the German department.
(4)   DB is a member of the German department.
(5)   DB will want a printer with a German character set.

In other words, you form an assumption in the expectation that you will be able to combine it with existing assumptions to derive a new assumption. Notice that the conclusion in (4) does not follow just from your observation of the pile of German books. It is a result of the interaction of the new assumption and other accessible assumptions. That is, it could be derived only in the *context* of the assumption in (2). This means that it is a context-dependent conclusion or, as Sperber and Wilson call it, a *contextual implication*. Using this terminology, we could say that you formed the assumption that there is a pile of German books on my desk in the expectation of deriving a contextual implication.

But recall that not all assumptions are held with the same degree of conviction. For example, the fact that my clock is ticking is not as good evidence for the assumption that it is correct as it is for the assumption that it is going. As we have seen, the strength of an assumption that is derived by inference can only be as strong as the weakest premise. Thus while you may hold the assumption that there is a pile of German books on my desk with a great deal of confidence, for someone to have German books on their desk is not by any means conclusive evidence that they are a member of the German department. Consequently, the conclusion in (4) cannot be held with complete confidence.

Let us return to our make-believe and now pretend that as you wait for me to finish my telephone call you hear me utter several phrases in what you believe to be German, and then you hear me utter the sentence in (6).

(6)   That won't fit in with the German department timetable.

Of course, you are not trying to listen to my conversation. Nevertheless, given the story so far, you will pay attention to my German phrases and the utterance in (6). Why? Because given certain other assumptions, they are further evidence for the assumption in (4). In other words, because they strengthen your confidence in an existing assumption.

But now let us suppose that as you try not to listen to my conversation you hear me say:

(7)   Yes, I'm glad I'm not a member of the German department.

Now what? This utterance entails the proposition in (8).

(8)   DB is not a member of the German department.

And this proposition is, of course, inconsistent with the assumption in (4). It is clear that you can't believe both. But equally it is clear which one you will reject – the one for which you have less evidence.

Let us end our story there and draw out its implications for the way we process information. The question was: given that we are capable of making all sorts of assumptions, why do we make the ones that we do? And the answer suggested by our story is: we form an assumption in the expectation that it will interact with our existing assumptions to yield what Sperber and Wilson call a *contextual effect*. We have identified three ways in which a new item of information may have a contextual effect:

1 It may allow the derivation of a contextual implication.
2 It may provide further evidence for, and hence strengthen, an existing assumption.
3 It may contradict an existing assumption.

When an item of information has a contextual effect in a given context, Sperber and Wilson say it is *relevant* in that context. In each case establishing the relevance of a new assumption involves inference. And in each case it involves the interaction of existing assumptions with new assumptions. The relevance of an assumption depends on the context in which it is processed. That, of course, was the point of Exercise 2.2.

But, surely, just about any assumption you might make has *some* contextual effect. For instance, there is probably some contextual effect that you can derive from the assumption in (9).

(9)   DB has some books on her desk.

And yet (in our story anyway) you are much more likely to derive the assumption in (10).

(10)   DB has some German books on her desk.

Why?

Intuitively, the answer is clear. Because in the scenario I've described (9) is much less relevant than (10). We are not just interested in obtaining relevant information. We are interested in obtaining the most relevant information. (That was the point of Exercise 2.1). It is tempting to think that this means obtaining information with the most contextual effects. The fact that the light goes on in my office when I press the switch has fewer contextual effects and is hence less relevant than the fact that it doesn't go on. However, if you were just interested in deriving as many contextual effects as possible from an assumption, then there would be nothing to stop you from continuing to process it, bringing more and more contextual information to bear on its interpretation.

Let me illustrate this problem with an artificial example. Suppose that on the basis of a perfectly reasonable contextual assumption (supply it for yourself) you derive (12) from your observation in (11).

(11) DB has a New Zealand accent.
(12) DB is from New Zealand.

As we have seen, an assumption stored in memory may give the hearer access to further information stored under a concept it contains. Supposing that your entry for *New Zealand* contains the information in (13), you will derive (14).

(13) New Zealand is the country where they grow kiwi fruit.
(14) DB comes from the country where they grow kiwi fruit

But now suppose that your entry for *kiwi fruit* contains (15).

(15) Kiwi fruit cost 18p each in Safeways.

This will enable you to derive (16), which combined with (17) will enable you to derive (18).

(16) DB is from the country where they grow the fruit that cost 18p each in Safeways.
(17) Safeways is Barbara's favourite store.
(18) DB is from the country where they grow the fruit that cost 18p each in Barbara's favourite store.

And so on.

Although processing could in principle go on for ever, it has to stop somewhere. But where? Intuitively, the answer is clear: where the processor thinks it is no longer worth the effort.

Processing information yields rewards (improvements to one's representation of the world) only at a cost. Deriving contextual effects takes time and effort, and the more time and effort expended the less relevant the information will seem. As this example has shown, each extension of the context involves a cost: the cost of accessing the assumption under *Safeways* is greater than the cost of accessing the assumption under *kiwi fruit*, which in turn is more costly to access than the assumption under *New Zealand*. Moreover, as the size of the context increases so does the cost of using the assumptions it contains. The inferences get more and more complex.

The suggestion is that in processing information people try to balance costs and rewards – they automatically process each new item of information in a context in which it yields a maximal contextual effect for a minimum cost in processing. This means that someone who is searching for relevance will extend the context only if the costs this entails seem more likely to be offset by contextual effects.

2.2   The Principle of Relevance

So far we have been talking about the way in which people process information that is, as it were, just lying there. In our story no one *communicated* the fact that there was a pile of German books on my desk. The books were just there. How, then, can this story help us in the explanation of the way people communicate?

I am assuming here that there is a clear difference between information that is communicated and information that is not. However, although we may have an intuitive idea of what counts as communication, philosophers have found it very difficult to develop these intuitions into a definition.[3] Perhaps the following exercises will help you see some of the problems involved:

Exercise 3

1   Is language always used for communication?

    (a)   Think of some examples of language use which you think do not involve communication.

    (b)   Discuss the example given by Chomsky:

> Once I had the curious experience of making a speech against the Vietnam war to a group of soldiers who were advancing in full combat gear, rifles in hand, to clear the area where I was speaking. I meant what I said – my statements had their strict and literal meaning – but this had little to do with my intentions at that moment. (1976: 61–2)

2   In his radio programme 'Viva Garibaldi', David Beane describes a young girl standing at the railing of a ship as it leaves Sicily. She continues to wave even when the buildings are mere dots. Is she communicating?

3   The scenario is much the same as that described earlier – you are waiting in my office to see me about my computing needs. The question in each of the following cases is: does it count as an instance of communication, and why/why not?

(a)   As you wait you fail to stifle a yawn.

(b)   As you wait you surreptitiously look at your watch, and I fail to notice.

(c)   You surreptitiously look at your watch, but I happen to see you.

(d)   As you wait you rearrange your papers so that the form from Computing Services becomes visible to me, but you do this in such a casual and natural way that (you hope) I do not recognize that you want me to see it.

(e)   You wave the form from Computing Services in the air and point to the clock.

Perhaps it is possible to extend the meaning of the word *communication* so that it covers 1 and 2. However, in doing so we would miss the opportunity to study one of the most important abilities underlying human interaction – the ability to attribute intentions to each other. Accordingly, we are going to require that for communication to take place there be a communicator and a (comprehending) audience. This means that talking to yourself, practising lines for a play, consecrating buildings and baptizing babies (to name just a few examples) are not instances of communication. It also means that (genuine) sneezing and yawning cannot be acts of communication. Communicative behaviour, in the sense being developed here, must be deliberate and involve intentions.

But what does a communicator intend? Suppose that you intend to communicate something by looking at your watch, but that I do not recognize this – I just think you want to know the time or that you are nervous. Since I do not recognize your intention to communicate, you will not have succeeded in doing so. But must you *intend* that I recognize your intention to communicate? What did you say about example (d) in Exercise 3.3 above? If it is communication, it is covert: the communicator is hiding his intention to communicate from the audience. In contrast, the intention in (e) is overt: the communicator intends that the audience recognize his intention to communicate.

This is where we come to our problem of definition. As Strawson (1964) and Schiffer (1972) have shown, there are examples which suggest that for communication to be fully overt the communicator must intend that the audience recognize that the communicator intends that the audience recognizes that he has the intention to communicate something, and still further examples which suggest that *this* intention must itself be recognized, and so on. The problem is to give a precise account of overt communication (and hence the intuitions underlying the distinctions in Exercise 3.3 above) in a way that is psychologically plausible – that is, in a way that does not require an infinite number of steps. Those readers whose heads are already spinning will be relieved to know that we are not going to attempt this here.[4] What is important for us is the significance of this property of communicative intentions. What difference does it make that the communicator's intention to communicate is evident to the audience? Why does someone who wants to communicate something bother making it known to the audience that he has this intention?

As we have seen in the last section, the aim in information processing is to recover as many contextual effects as possible for the least cost in processing. That is, the aim is to balance costs and rewards. However, when you attend to a phenomenon that has not been deliberately communicated (for example, the pile of German books on my desk or my accent), there is no guarantee that your efforts will be rewarded. You will only have hopes of a satisfactory degree of relevance. In contrast, if you recognize that I am deliberately trying to attract your attention (for example, by pointing to the pile of books or exaggerating my New Zealand accent), then you will not just have hopes that your efforts will be rewarded, but expectations. In other words, an act of (overt) communication brings with it a presumption that there is information worth processing.

Why? The answer lies in another question. What would be the point in my spending effort in attracting your attention if I didn't think I had any information that was relevant to you? What would be the point of my deliberately wasting your processing effort? The answer is, of course, either none at all (in which case I would be irrational) or my aim is something other than communication (as it has been defined here). You might like to think about filibustering or Chomsky's example in the exercise above.

This is not to say that a communicator always does have information that is worth the audience's attention. Suppose, for example, that as you enter a lecture hall you see an empty seat behind me, but I don't recognize that you have seen it. In this case it is not really worth your paying attention to my gestures: you already have the information that I am trying to communicate. Communication takes place at a risk, and the grounds on which a speaker bases his assumption that his utterance is worth processing may be mistaken.

Exercise 4

1   (Not for New Zealand readers!) Suppose that you are a participant in a
    conversation which includes the following exchange:

A: Did you ever go surfing when you were in New Zealand?
B: We were living in Taihape.

Is B's response sufficiently relevant to you? What is the problem?

2   Which is the most relevant answer to A's question below?

A: What happened at work today?
B: Oh, the usual.
B': I got fired.

Would a speaker necessarily give the most relevant answer? Why/why not?

3   What factors contribute towards B's choice to answer as in (a) rather than (b)?

    A: Would you like something to eat?
(a) B: I've just had lunch actually.
(b) B: No.

Now, as we have seen, the hearer is not just interested in obtaining some reward. Her aim is to achieve the greatest contextual possible effect for the available processing effort. This means that it is in her interests that the information presented is the most relevant information available to the communicator. But of course a communicator will have his own aims and interests, and these may lead him to give the audience information whose effect is less than that of other information that he could have given (see Exercise 4.2 above). Nevertheless, to be worth the audience's attention it must have some effect.

We have also seen that accessing contextual information and using it to derive contextual effects involves a cost (time and effort), and that the cost of deriving contextual effects in a small, easily accessible context will be less than the cost of obtaining them in a larger, less accessible context. This means that it is in the audience's interests that the communicator should produce an utterance whose interpretation calls for less effort than any other utterance he could have made to achieve the same effect. There are always a number of ways of conveying the same information, and these may require different amounts of effort from the hearer. Consider, for example, the sequences in (19) and (20) (taken from Blass 1990: 85–6).

(19)   He went to McDonald's. The quarter pounder sounded good and he ordered it.
(20)   The river had been dry for a long time. Everyone attended the funeral.

Blass assumes that while the first sequence would present little difficulty for a Westerner, the second would seem incomprehensible. The problem is that for a Western reader there is no connection between the two segments of (20). That is, there is nothing conveyed by the first that could be used in interpreting the second. In contrast, for a speaker of Sissala (a Niger-Congo language spoken in Burkina Faso and Ghana) the sequence in (19) would yield no contextual effect while the one in (20) would be perfectly comprehensible.

A Western speaker who wanted to communicate the information in (19) to a Sissala speaker would have to make the required contextual assumptions explicit – for example, by producing the sequence in (21). On the other hand, a Sissala speaker who wanted to communicate the information in (20) to a Westerner would have to produce a sequence like (22).

(21)   He went to a place where food is prepared and cooked called McDo-
       nald's. There he saw ground meat which is formed into patties, fried and
       placed between two pieces of bread.
(22)   If a river has been dry a long time, then a river spirit has died. Whenever
       a spirit dies there is a funeral. The river had been dry for a long time.

Obviously, these sequences are much more complex than the corresponding ones in (19) and (20). However, the complexity is the price the speaker must pay to ensure successful communication. In other words, they provide the most relevant means for communicating the information in question. Notice that the sequence in (21) would be far less relevant to a Westerner than the one in (19). The extra effort spent in processing it would not be offset by an increase in contextual effects. Similarly, a Sissala speaker would find (22) much less relevant than (20).

Of course no Western speaker who wished to communicate with another would have produced the sequence in (21) in the first place. Assuming that he does want to communicate, it is in his interest to make his utterance as easily understood as possible. Indeed, any Western hearer presented with (21) might doubt that genuine communication was intended and refuse to make the processing effort required. The same point applies to the Sissala example.

In other words, the presumption of relevance carried by every act of overt communication has two aspects: on the one hand, it creates a presumption of adequate effect, while on the other it creates a presumption of minimally necessary effort. Taken together, these presumptions define a level of *optimal relevance* – a presumption that the utterance will have adequate contextual effects for the minimum necessary processing. Sperber and Wilson call the principle that gives rise to the presumption of optimal relevance *the principle of relevance*.

This means that a hearer is entitled to go ahead and interpret every utterance in the expectation that it is optimally relevant. She may, of course, be disappointed in her expectation. The speaker may be only pretending to communicate (remember filibustering). And even speakers who are genuinely trying to communicate may succeed in only boring or baffling their audiences. Moreover, hearers do not always actually accept that the presumption carried by an act of communication is true. The speaker's previous record as a bore or a baffler may lead the hearer to doubt his ability to succeed in being relevant. (How many times have you 'turned off' at the sound of a familiar voice?)

Communication takes place at a risk, and if a speaker is understood to be taking that risk, then he will be taken to be communicating his intention that the hearer believes that his utterance is relevant. Even boring or baffling speakers intend their audiences to believe that they are worth listening to.

As the examples in (19) and (20) show, what counts as optimal relevance varies according to the contextual resources of the speaker. It also varies with the way in which information is made accessible. While some utterances have to be processed immediately if the hearer is to obtain any contextual effects at all, other utterances, for example, those that are part of a book, are accessible and relevant for a longer time. It may be irritating for someone to interrupt you now to tell you that your tea is ready, but the speaker is not necessarily being irrelevant.

This is not to say that it is not relevant for a writer or speaker to remind the hearer of information that he has already made accessible. If I think that I cannot reasonably expect you to access information that is necessary for the interpretation of an utterance or sequence of utterances, then it will be relevant for me to remind you of it. Consider how often a writer or lecturer prefaces his utterances with 'As we have seen' or 'Recall that'. Indeed, it seems that the relevance of some utterances lies entirely in the way they provide contexts for the interpretation of subsequent utterances. Consider, for example, the opening sentences of novels.

What counts as optimal relevance also varies according to the hearer's processing abilities or intellectual awareness. Compare, for example, the effort you are prepared to put into processing utterances which are part of a conversation at a party with the effort you put into understanding a lecture. As we all know, some speakers get it wrong and their audiences feel patronized. Others treat their audiences as if they were omniscient geniuses. However, as I have said, Sperber and Wilson's claim is not that speakers always succeed in being optimally relevant, but rather that they intend their audiences to believe that they have achieved optimal relevance. The aim of this book is to show that this is enough to explain how utterances are understood.

Recommended Reading

Communication

Sperber and Wilson 1986: ch 1, see especially pp. 46–60; 1987 (précis of Sperber and Wilson 1986 and authors' response to Open Peer Commentary).
Grice 1989: 213.
Strawson 1964.

Grice's Maxims of Conversation

Grice 1975; 1989: 1–37.
Wilson and Sperber 1981 (a critique of Grice).
Levinson 1983: ch. 3 (an outline of Grice's theory of conversation).

Relevance and the Principle of Relevance

Sperber and Wilson 1986: ch. 3; 1987 (see above).
Contributions by: Clark, Levinson, McCawley, Morgan and Green, Russell, Hinkelman, Wilks, Bach and Harnish in Open Peer Commentary on Sperber and Wilson (1986) in *Behavioural and Brain Sciences*, 10, 697–754.
Pateman 1986 (a review of Sperber and Wilson 1986).

Notes

1 I am grateful to Andrew Spencer for this example.
2 This is a written version of part of Grice's William James lectures delivered in 1967.
3 See, for example, Grice (1957), Searle (1969), Schiffer (1972), Recanati (1986, 1987). For Sperber and Wilson's approach to the problem see their chapter 1.
4 But those readers familiar with the problem as it is approached by Strawson and Schiffer may be interested to see how Sperber and Wilson use the notion of *mutual manifestness* to develop an alternative psychologically plausible approach (chapter 1, especially sections 4, 6, 8, 9, 12). For a critique of Sperber and Wilson's approach see Recanati (1986, 1987).

3 Pragmatics, Linguistics and Literature

3.1 Carving up Meaning: Semantics and Pragmatics

The search for relevance is something that constrains all communication, verbal and non-verbal. However, this book is about the way people understand utterances, and utterances have linguistic properties and non-linguistic properties. Since an utterance consists of a certain sentence or phrase with a certain syntactic structure and made up of words with certain meanings, its interpretation will depend on the hearer's linguistic knowledge. However, since it is produced by a particular speaker on a particular occasion and the hearer's task is to discover what that speaker meant on that occasion, its interpretation will also depend on the non-linguistic knowledge that she brings to bear. Our task is to show how the principle of relevance explains the interaction between these two types of knowledge in the interpretation of utterances.

The assumption underlying this task and, indeed, the whole discussion so far is that there is a distinction between a hearer's knowledge of her language and her knowledge of the world. In this section I shall argue that it is this distinction that underlies the distinction between *semantics* and *pragmatics*. Many readers will be aware of the controversies surrounding this distinction. As Recanati (1987:19) points out, there are many respects in which these controversies are terminological – that is, controversies over what we should call semantics and what we should call pragmatics. While there does not seem to be much point in devoting space to that sort of issue, it does seem worthwhile discussing the grounds on which distinctions within a general theory of utterance interpretation should be drawn.[1]

I have already indicated that this book is concerned with communication from a cognitive point of view. This means that we shall be interested in distinctions that are grounded in human psychology, or, in other words, that we shall be drawing the distinction between semantics and pragmatics within the domain of human psychology. This distinguishes our approach, first, from those approaches that are not interested in human cognition at all, and, second, from those approaches whose interest in communication is restricted to its social aspects. Obviously, you don't have to be interested in human cognition. However, as we shall see, many of the problems addressed by non-psychological approaches to communication presuppose answers to the issues we have been discussing here.

The assumption that there is a distinction between linguistic and non-linguistic knowledge marks our approach as *modular*, and thus as consistent with the view of language found in Chomskyan generative grammar.[2] According to this approach, knowledge of language is one of a system of interacting modules which make up the mind, each of which has its own particular properties. This implies that the mind does not develop as a whole, but with specific capacities developing in their own ways and in their own time. In other words, knowledge of language cannot be regarded as the result of general intelligence.[3] It also implies that actual linguistic performance – that is, the way we use language – is a result of the interaction of a number of different systems, and that the acceptability of an utterance may be affected by factors other than its grammatical well-formedness. An utterance may consist of a perfectly grammatical sentence and still be unacceptable. Equally, an ungrammatical sentence may be used in the production of a perfectly acceptable utterance.

Exercise 1

Discuss whether any of the following are unacceptable, and if so whether the unacceptability is grammatical.

(a) My uncle considers that himself is a genius.
(b) My toothbrush considers itself to be a genius.
(c) My father has no children.
(d) My father have no children.
(e) My toothbrush has no children.
(f) You can't do that can't you?
(g) I'm very happy aren't I?
(h) Tom eats pears and fruit.
(i) My grandmother wrote me a letter yesterday and six men can fit into the back seat of a Ford. (Gleitman 1965)
(j) He slept and got into bed.

Grammatical well-formedness, we are saying, is independent of what we know about the world: if a sentence is ungrammatical, it is ungrammatical in every context. While there is no space here to discuss in detail the empirical grounds for saying that grammatical knowledge is independent of world knowledge, we should say something about the ways in which they differ.

It is assumed that within the framework of generative grammar certain sound sequences are assigned various levels of representation – phonological, syntactic and logical – which are related to each other by a system of linguistic rules or computations. While this system of rules may provide the basis for the propositional knowledge that such and such a sequence is or is not a grammatical sentence of the language in question, it cannot itself be characterized in terms of a set of propositional knowledge statements. For example, while I may be said to know *that* the sentence in (1) is ungrammatical in much the same way that I may be said to know that oak trees are deciduous, I may not be said to have this sort of (propositional) knowledge of the binding principles which provide the basis for my grammaticality judgement.[4]

(1)   Jane believes Simon to admire herself.

For a start, I may not be said to *believe* these principles (or, indeed, any other principles of grammar) – at least not in the sense of conscious belief.[5] Grammatical representations are not the sort of representations that are taken as the objects of propositional attitudes. Further, although a grammatical representation is a representation of something – that is, the sound sequence that caused it – it cannot be said to be true or false in the way that a propositional representation is. As Chomsky puts it, 'The question of truth, conformity to an external reality, does not enter in the way it does in connection with our knowledge of the properties of objects' (1980: 27).[6]

However, while linguistic representations may not themselves be truth-bearing, it is clear that the grammar provides one of the means for acquiring true or false representations of the world. As we have seen, our beliefs and assumptions about the world are acquired not only through natural language but also through the various perceptual systems. For example, I may be told that it's raining or I may discover it for myself by looking out of the window. Either way the assumption I acquire may be true or false. That is, either way it has truth conditions.

But linguists aren't interested in the truth or falsity of what we believe. They are concerned with the truth and falsity of what we say. Why? Because there is a connection between the meaning of what we say and truth, a connection that has been explored in the development of *truth-conditional semantics*. The basic idea here is: knowing the meaning of a sentence is a matter of knowing what the world would have to be like for it to be true. For example, to know the meaning of (2) is to know that it is true if and only if tigers eat grass.

(2)   Tigers eat grass.

It doesn't matter that you don't know whether in fact tigers eat grass. The point is that if you know the meaning of the sentence, then you could assign it a truth value depending on what the world was like. [7]

But as truth-conditional semanticists themselves have recognized, in the vast majority of cases it is impossible to assign truth conditions to *sentences*. I had to choose my example in (2) very carefully. If I had chosen any of the sentences below, then I wouldn't have been able to say what the truth conditions were.

(3) I arrived yesterday.
(4) Nellie tripped over her trunk.
(5) That is too hot.
(6) Everyone is.

The problem in each case is that we cannot assign truth conditions unless we have more information. For example, in (6) we need to know the domain of the quantifier (for example, everyone in the room) and what property is being predicated. In (5) we have to know what *that* refers to, which sense of *hot* is being intended, and what whatever it is is too hot for. This information is, of course, non-linguistic information, and according to the modular view of the mind just described, this means that the assignment of truth conditions is not a matter for the grammar at all.

However, many truth-conditional semanticists have proposed that the grammar be extended so that it assigns truth conditions not to sentences but to sentence–context pairs.[8] On this approach the context is simply a specification of the identity of the speaker, the audience, the time and place of utterance, the identification of any indicated objects and whatever else is needed. What is needed is determined by the grammar. Thus the use of *I* indicates that the context must include information about the speaker, the use of *yesterday* indicates that it must include information about the time of utterance. So if the context includes the information that the speaker is Diane and today is 23 October 1989, then we shall know that (3) is true if and only if Diane arrived on 22 October 1989.

In this case the hearer happens to be directed to a unique context and hence a unique interpretation. *I* means the speaker and *yesterday* means the day before the day the utterance was made, and in both cases there will be only one referent meeting the description on a given occasion. But when we turn to sentences containing demonstratives like *this* we have a problem deciding what information should be included in the context. For there is invariably more than one object that the speaker could have intended. Even pointing doesn't necessarily help. Consider how you would interpret the following two utterances made by a speaker pointing to a carton of milk.

(7)   This is good for you.
(8)   This is made from trees.

Exercise 2

Explain why the meaning of *here* does not direct the hearer to a context which enables her to recover a unique interpretation for the following:

> She brought it here.

What these examples show is that the context for the interpretation of an utterance cannot be fixed in advance, as for example Lewis (1972) proposes, but must be constructed as part of the process of interpreting it. As Lewis himself comes to recognize (1979), the hearer's aim is to choose the context which yields an acceptable interpretation of the utterance.[9] But unless we are able to specify what makes an utterance acceptable, we cannot say what the hearer's goal in selecting and using the context is.

According to the arguments of chapters 1 and 2, the solution to this problem takes us out of the domain of a grammar which pairs symbols and meanings and into the domain of a general theory of cognition. That is, the interpretation of utterances containing indexical expression involves cognitive processes which are involved in the acquisition of beliefs and assumptions from other sources (for example, vision) and which are constrained by a principle that applies to both verbal and non-verbal communication. This is true of *all* contextually determined aspects of propositional content, including those which are not treated by truth-conditional semantics – for example, disambiguation, the resolution of vagueness, reference assignment and the recovery of ellipsed material.

Does this mean, as Gazdar (1979: 2) warns us, that natural languages will not have a semantics but only a syntax and a pragmatics?[10] If semantics is defined (as it is by Gazdar) as a theory of the way truth conditions are assigned, then the answer has to be yes. For as we have seen, this cannot be part of the grammar. But this is not to say that semanticists no longer have a job. The meanings of linguistic expressions and constructions obviously do play a role in utterance interpretation. Moreover, this includes playing a role in the determination of truth conditions. Linguistic (semantic) properties of sentences like those in (3) to (6) only determine *blueprints* for propositions. The problem for semantics is to specify the properties of these blueprints and to explain how they are arrived at. The task for pragmatics is to show how the hearer is able to develop such a blueprint into a complete proposition on the basis of contextual knowledge.

In fact, according to Gazdar's definition, the semanticist's job is more restricted than it is according to the definition being adopted here. For there are many aspects of linguistic meaning which cannot be explained in terms of truth conditions.

First, since according to standard truth-conditional analyses the differences between the (a) and the (b) examples in (9) and (10) are not differences in truth-conditional content, the role of the underlined performative expressions and of the imperative and interrogative mood would have to be studied outside semantics.

(9) (a) *I warn you* that Nigel is coming.
     (b) *I assure you* that Nigel is coming.
(10) (a) Are you being helpful?
     (b) Be helpful.
     (c) You are being helpful.

Many readers will recognize these examples as the property of speech act theory, which is often said to be a central part of pragmatics (see, for example, Stalnaker (1972), Bach and Harnish (1979), Levinson (1983)). We shall be reassessing the assumptions of this approach in chapter 6. To assign the phenomena in (9) and (10) to pragmatics on the grounds that they are not truth-conditional is to obscure the relationship between linguistic form and interpretation. Devices like mood do not fully determine an interpretation. There are, for example, contexts in which the speaker of (10c) would be understood to be asking the hearer whether she is being helpful even though the indicative mood is associated with assertion. In other words, the hearer has to use the linguistic clue provided by the speaker in conjunction with contextual information. The semanticist's and the pragmatist's jobs interact.

For someone wanting to maintain a truth-conditional approach to semantics it is very important that there be a non-semantic explanation for those aspects of linguistic meaning that do not contribute to truth conditions. Not surprisingly, this has influenced and shaped the preoccupations of pragmatic theorizing. Some writers (for example, Gazdar (1979), Horn (1972, 1983) and Levinson (1987)) have been concerned to find a pragmatic explanation for the fact that utterances containing logical operators may carry suggestions which are not part of their meanings as they are defined in logic. For instance, that (11b) is generally conveyed by the utterance in (11a) might seem to suggest that the natural language quantifiers are not equivalent to their logical counterparts $\exists x$ and $\forall x$, since it is impossible to derive this suggestion on the basis of the logical definitions of the logical quantifiers.

(11) (a)   Some of the students were there.
      (b)   Not all of the students were there.

Similarly, the oddity of (12) might seem to suggest that natural language *and* can mean *and then* and is not equivalent to the natural language connective *&*.

(12)   ?She rode off and got on her bicycle.

Significantly, the argument that these phenomena are not semantic consists in a demonstration that they can be explained in non-linguistic terms. That is, it is shown that the suggestion in (11b) is not due to the meaning of *some*, but to general communicative principles. At the same time, however, it is usually claimed that these suggestions are *generalized*. That is, they are normally carried by the utterance and are cancelled only in specific circumstances. In this respect they differ from those *particularized* kinds of contextual implications discussed earlier – for example, the suggestion conveyed by B's response in the following exchange.

(13)   A: Are you hungry?
       B: I've just had lunch at Anne's.

The suggestion is that whereas we can develop a procedure for predicting when suggestions carried by utterances like (11a) are recovered, there can be no such procedure for examples like (13) since the interpretation depends on idio-syncratic features of the context and cannot be predicted by a general rule – is Anne a generous hostess or notoriously mean? In other words, on this approach the kind of pragmatic explanation we need for maintaining a truth-conditional theory of semantics in the face of examples like (11) and (12) is quite different from the kind of pragmatic explanation we need for examples like (13).

However, since the interpretation of both sorts of examples involves the same ingredients – the linguistic form of the utterance, contextual assumptions and the assumption that the speaker is being relevant – a theory which treated the examples in (11) and (12) differently from the one in (13) would seem to be in danger of missing important generalizations. If there is a principle that constrains the interaction of linguistic and non-linguistic knowledge in the interpretation of utterances, this principle would have to operate in the interpretation of both types of example. This issue will be taken up again in chapters 4 and 5.

Whatever the shape the explanation for the examples in (11) and (12) takes, it is certainly pragmatic – that is, non-linguistic. As we shall see, there are convincing arguments that the suggestions carried by utterances containing *some* and *and* are not due to the meanings of these words. This is not to say, however, that there are not examples of words and structures whose contribution to the interpretation of the utterances that contain them cannot be explained in truth-conditional terms. For example, it is evident that the difference between the (a) and the (b) example in (14) is due to the differences in their word order.

(14)   (a)   It was in October that Nigel told me.
       (b)   It was Nigel who told me in October

But this difference is not a truth-conditional one: they are true under exactly the same circumstances.

Similarly, all the utterances in (16) are true under the same conditions, and yet each would be interpreted as a different response to the utterance in (15).

(15)   Anne is coming.
(16)   (a)   So Nigel's here.
       (b)   After all Nigel's here.
       (c)   Moreover Nigel's here.
       (d)   However Nigel's here.

This is not the place to analyse the interpretation of these utterances. The point is simply that the differences are due to the meanings of the words with which they are prefaced.[11]

Obviously, these examples are a problem for an approach which aims to define linguistic meaning in terms of truth conditions. The only solution would seem to be to consign them to pragmatics. However, while it is true that the meanings of these expressions play a role in the way that contextual assumptions are used in the interpretation of the utterances that contain them, there is no reason for saying that this role is itself pragmatically determined. The knowledge of what these words mean is linguistic knowledge, and, as we have seen, this is quite different from the non-linguistic knowledge that a hearer brings to bear on the interpretation of an utterance. In other words, the meanings of these expressions can be represented in pragmatics only at the expense of the modular view of cognition described above.

It is clear, then, that if the job of the semanticist is to describe the meanings of those linguistic expressions and constructions that play a role in utterance interpretation, then she has plenty to do. There is no danger of any language being left without a semantics. On the other hand, if the semanticist is to say what role these expressions and constructions play, then she cannot afford to overlook the role of non-linguistic knowledge in utterance interpretation and the principles which constrain its use. It is in this sense that pragmatics underlies the study of linguistic semantics.

While this conception of pragmatics might be regarded as too all-encompassing by some, others might regard it as too narrow. For example, the domain of what Leech (1983) calls 'General Pragmatics' includes something called 'Socio-pragmatics', a theory which studies the effect of socially determined maxims or principles. Consequently, the study of the interaction between grammar and pragmatics includes the study of phenomena which are sometimes regarded as belonging to the domain of sociolinguistics – for example, the effect of social distance on language choice. [12]

Leech (1983: 6) defines pragmatics as 'meaning in relation to speech situations', a definition which, at first, might seem to be based on the distinction that we have been underlining – that is, the distinction between linguistic and non-linguistic knowledge. And, indeed, Leech argues that grammar must be separated from pragmatics. However, a 'speech situation' is not a psychological construct since it includes elements that are defined objectively, independently of the speaker and hearer. 'Background knowledge' is only one aspect of the speech situation. More importantly, the 'goals of an utterance', another element in the speech situation, are constrained by social maxims. In other words, the distinction between semantics and pragmatics is not drawn within the domain of cognitive psychology.

As I have said, there is no reason why the study of the social aspects of communication should be ruled out by a psychological theory of utterance interpretation. The question is whether the study of phenomena such as politeness or the distribution of talk among the participants in a conversation can contribute towards an explanation of the very possibility of communication between human beings. We have seen that what speakers say may indeed be governed by social or cultural factors. And in such cases the success of the communication will depend on the hearer's ability to supply assumptions about the relevant social institutions and relationships. However, we still need, as we do with any case of utterance interpretation, an explanation of how these assumptions are selected and used. Equally, while it is true that a speaker may use language in order to communicate his beliefs and assumptions about social relationships (for example, between himself and the hearer), we still need to explain how the hearer's linguistic knowledge (the grammatical rules encoding these relationships) interacts with her non-linguistic knowledge for the successful interpretation of the utterance.

In other words, there is no conflict between Leech's socio-pragmatic approach and the present psychological approach because they are attempting to do different things. For this reason it is misleading to include phenomena like politeness, face-saving and turn taking together with the phenomena discussed in the following chapters under the general heading of pragmatics.

The issue is not just about what we should *call* pragmatics, but that this conflation obscures the fact that these two approaches are doing different things, and, more particularly, that the study of 'socio-pragmatic' phenomena depends on answers to the sort of questions that were discussed in chapter 2.

3.2   Promises and Poetry

Some readers may think that I have forgotten the promise I made in section 1.1. After agreeing that communication could and would not be regarded simply as the transmission of facts, I went on to discuss it as if it were just that. I may have mentioned propositional attitudes now and then, but I have hardly done justice to the full range of uses to which language may be put, and I have avoided the cases mentioned at the end of section 1.1, where what the speaker communicates is not propositional at all. Inevitably, at this stage of the book I am going to be making more promises. However, I would like to conclude this chapter by trying to put the issues raised by those examples into some sort of theoretical perspective. There is no space here for either detailed exposition or fully argued criticism. My aim is simply to indicate how the framework being developed here differs from others in its approach to the fact, first, that language can be used for making promises (and issuing warnings, placing bets and giving orders), and, second, that language can be used for poetry (and poetic prose).

In making a promise (or in issuing a warning or giving an order) one is not describing an existing state of affairs, but rather creating a new one. More specifically, one is creating a new social relationship. Accordingly, the philosopher J. L. Austin (1962) argued that for a better understanding of language we need an explanation of the way language is embedded in social institutions and of the various actions it can be used to perform. In other words, we need to view language as a vehicle for social action rather than as a vehicle for thought. The assumption underlying this view is that when a speaker communicates he communicates the fact that he is performing an act of a certain type, and communication is successful only if the hearer identifies the type of act being performed. So when I make a promise I communicate the fact that I am making a promise and you will understand my utterance only if you recognize that I was making a promise. Similarly, when I issue a warning you must recognize my utterance as a warning in order to understand it. In other words, the classification and identification of *speech acts* plays an essential role in communication.

As we shall see in chapter 6, this assumption is not always justified. However, it happens to be true in the case of promises. If you hadn't recognized that I had promised to show how poetic utterances can be accommodated in this framework, then you would have missed the relevance of my remarks at the end of section 1.1. For a start, you would not have recognized that you were entitled to chastise me had I continued to ignore poetic utterances. Moreover, it is clear that your understanding of the implications of my remarks hinged on your understanding of the social institution of promising: you know that if someone makes a promise, they are morally obliged to keep it.

But does this necessarily mean that communication must be seen in terms of social interaction? Let us change the example and say that I have promised to lend you my French dictionary. If you understand my utterance, then you will recover the assumption in (17).

(17)   DB is promising to lend me her French dictionary.

Given your understanding of what promising is, you will recover certain contextual implications – for example the ones in (18).

(18)   (a)   DB is morally obliged to lend me her French dictionary.
       (b)   If DB does not lend me her French dictionary, then I am entitled to reprimand her.

But are the processes involved here different from those involved in the interpretation of any other utterance? On the basis of the linguistic clue provided by my utterance and the context, you recover the assumption in (17), and given your contextual assumptions about promising, you derive the contextual implications in (18). At every stage your interpretation is constrained by your assumption that my utterance is optimally relevant. It is true that the contextual assumptions you used to establish the relevance of my utterance were about the social institution of promising, and it is true that a psychological approach to utterance interpretation cannot tell you anything about that. Moreover, it is true that we have developed formulae for dealing with certain social and cultural institutions (for example, *How's that* (cricket), *I bid no trumps* (bridge), *I name this ship Maggie*. However, we still need a theory which explains how a hearer uses contextual information (whatever its source) to establish the relevance of any utterance, and from the point of view of this theory the fact that you used institutional or social knowledge in the interpretation of an utterance is 'no more and no less interesting than the fact that in order to discover by looking out of the window that rain is on the way some meterological knowledge is required' (Sperber and Wilson 1985).

Earlier I suggested that language may be seen either as a vehicle for action (the speech-act-theory view) or as a vehicle for thought. But, of course, that is a simplification. We do not just communicate our thoughts. We communicate our desires, our regrets, our fears, our doubts, our worries and our delight. Moreover, the attitude that a speaker conveys may be indicated either non-linguistically – for example I may say something in a sad tone of voice – or linguistically, as in (19).

(19)   (a)   Unfortunately she has missed the train.
       (b)   Thank goodness she has missed the train.

Inasmuch as a speaker may communicate by his utterance that he is sad that P or that he is delighted that P, there is no problem. The hearer recovers these assumptions and establishes their relevance. However, as we have seen, what the speaker communicates by his utterance is not always as specific as this. He may communicate an impression of sadness or an impression of delight. But what sort of thing is an impression? And how does one establish its relevance?

   Although this is a problem raised by all types of communication, it has really been addressed only by those interested in the interpretation of literary texts. For example, Coleridge (1906: 263) points out that once it is recognized that 'language is framed to convey not the object alone, but likewise the character, mood and intentions of the person who is representing it' then it should not be surprising that the test of a 'blameless style' is its 'untranslatableness in words of the same language without injury to the meaning'.

   Applying this to our example in chapter 1 (repeated below), there is no single meaning that Shakespeare wished to convey by Emilia's utterance.

(20)   'Tis not a year or two but show us a man,
       They are all but stomachs and we all but food,
       They eat us hungerly, and when they are full,
       They belch us.

Did Emilia simply mean that men exploit women? While it is clear that this is not an adequate paraphrase of her utterance, it is less clear what exactly it fails to capture. Emilia's anger? Her disgust? There is a whole range of impressions and emotions conveyed by this utterance, and hence it is misleading to say that there is a single meaning Emilia intended the hearer to recover. We cannot point to a specific proposition and say '*That* is the real meaning.'

   But if there is no translation of this utterance in terms of the literal, then there is, as Butler (1984: 20) puts it, 'no point at which interpretation may reasonably stop'. Indeed, as Butler goes on to say, it suggests that there is no notion of literality at all, no relationship between language and reality.

This is essentially the conclusion reached by Shelley who argued that the language of poets is 'vitally metaphorical', and that 'if no new poets should arise to create afresh the associations which have been . . . disorganized, language will be dead to all the nobler purposes of human intercourse' (1820: 26). More recently, Derrida has argued that even the language of philosophy, which one might expect to be as literal as possible, is full of the 'white mythology of hidden metaphor' (1974 :9). But if this is right, and if, as Lakoff and Johnson (1980) have argued, metaphor pervades ordinary language, then all interpretation is condemned to indeterminacy. In particular, we cannot talk about metaphor except in metaphorical terms. Thus we have statements like

Metaphor is the dreamwork of language. (Davidson 1979: 29)

Examine language; what, if you except some elements of natural sound, what is it all but metaphors recognized as such or no longer recognized; still fluid and florid or now solid-grown and colourless? If these same primitive garments are the osseous fixtures of the Flesh-Garment language, then are metaphors its muscle and living integuments. (S. J. Brown, in Ortony 1979: 20)

While literary theorists have accepted that 'no critic can claim to have seized absolutely the author's meaning' (Ray, 1984: 2), in pragmatics, writers have persisted in assuming that there is a meaning to be recovered, that the communicator intends to convey a specific set of assumptions. In view of examples like (20) and the other examples discussed in chapter 1, it seems that pragmatics would do well to follow the example of literary theory and accommodate the vague cases of communication within an overall theory of communication. On the other hand, these types of communication do not necessarily have to be explained in vague terms. Nor does the fact that there is no single interpretation for a text or utterance mean that interpretation is not constrained at all. Speakers do not just say anything and expect to be understood, and hearers do not recover just any interpretation for an utterance. As we shall see, in some cases the hearer is given considerable responsibility for interpretation so that an utterance conveys a wide range of assumptions, while in other cases the speaker's intentions are more specific. Indeterminacy is a matter of degree. But in all cases the hearer is constrained by her search for relevance.

According to this view, there is no sharp dividing line between the metaphorical and the literal. The same cognitive processes are involved in understanding all utterances. This distinguishes our view from the classical (Aristotelian) view of figurative language where figurative utterances crucially involve a departure from a norm, and brings us close to the more recent theories of literary meaning where the distinction between the metaphorical and the literal does not exist. However, this does not mean that we cannot have an explanatory theory of the role of figurative language in communication.

Anyone who regarded metaphor as a departure from the norm of literal speaking would be committed to saying that it played no role in communication, or, at least, no role other than that of mere decoration. For example, according to Aristotle, literal language is there to 'secure the requisite clearness' while figurative language is there to save communication from seeming 'mean and prosaic' (1940: 59). In contrast, according to the view presented in this book, metaphor does contribute to what is communicated. What is communicated cannot be regarded as a specific assumption or set of assumptions. This means that style cannot be thought of as something on top of or in addition to meaning. If we must describe metaphor in metaphorical terms, then we should not use the metaphor used by Whitman in the following:

> He [the greatest poet] says to his art, I will not be meddlesome, I will not have in my writing any elegance or effect or originality to hang in the way between me and the rest like curtains. I will have nothing hang in the way, not the richest curtains. What I tell I tell for precisely what it is. (Preface to 1855 edition of *Leaves of Grass*; quoted by Sontag 1987: 16)

As Sontag comments, 'practically all metaphors for style amount to placing matter on the inside, style on the outside. It would be more to the point to reverse the metaphor' (1987: 17).

Of course, metaphor is not the only dimension of poetic style, and poetic style is not the only dimension of style. If decisions about style are decisions about the linguistic form of one's utterance, then no one – writer or speaker, poet or accountant – can avoid making them. Obviously, some speakers/ writers devote more time and effort to stylistic choices than others. But if he is aiming at optimal relevance, then any speaker must make assumptions about the hearer's processing abilities and contextual resources, and these assumptions will be reflected in the form of his utterance.

Recommended Reading

The Pragmatics-Semantics Distinction

Sperber and Wilson 1986: 3–15.
Levinson 1983: 5–35; 1989.
Gazdar 1979: 1–7.
Recanati 1987: 1–20.

Speech Acts and Poetic Effects

See Recommended Reading for chapters 6 and 9.

Notes

1 For a survey of the various uses of the term *pragmatics* see Levinson (1983).
2 See J. A. Fodor (1983) for a detailed argument for the modularity of the human mind. For a very clear introduction to the issues surrounding modularity see Carston (1988a).
3 Cf. Piaget. For further discussion see Chomsky (1986), Newmeyer (1983), Lightfoot 1983 and Carston (1988a).
4 For an introduction to these principles see Haegeman (1991).
5 For a discussion of this issue see Davies (1989).
6 This has led some philosophers to criticize Chomsky for talking of knowledge of language at all. Certainly, knowledge of the rules and representation of language could not be described as true justified belief. However, as Chomsky (1980) has pointed out, this traditional definition of knowledge itself receives little support from either ordinary usage or general epistemological considerations. See Gettier (1963). In any case, it is clear that knowledge of grammar cannot be reduced to knowing how. It crucially involves a system of mental representations and computations. If the fact that these representations are not truth-bearing disqualifies them from being known, then we can always follow Chomsky's example and use the term *cognize* instead.
7 For an introduction to truth-conditional semantics see Kempson (1977) and J.D. Fodor (1977).
8 D. Lewis (1972), who adopts this approach, calls his theory indexical semantics, while Montague (1974) refers to his programme as pragmatics. Notice that Montague's conception of pragmatics is very different from the one being developed here.
9 We shall be returning to this point in chapter 5.
10 This warning is also found in Levinson's (1989) review of Sperber and Wilson (1986). He concludes that according to Sperber and Wilson 'virtually all the pre-occupations of modern theoretical semanticists will lie outside semantics proper; indeed they will not be distinguished from general thought processes, let alone from pragmatics' – a conclusion which he considers to be 'unnatural and unnecessary' (pp. 468–9).
11 For further discussion see section 8.2.
12 For another example of an approach which includes the study of social factors which influence language choice, see Green (1989).

Part II Explicature

4 Explicating and Implicating

A single utterance conveys a whole variety of assumptions. Some of these may have been specifically intended by the speaker. Others may fall within a range of assumptions intended by the speaker. In some cases the speaker's intention is overt, in others it is covert, and in others an assumption is conveyed completely by accident.

In this part of the book we shall be only concerned with those assumptions that the speaker intends to convey. Moreover, we are concerned only with those cases in which the speaker does not hide his intention to convey certain assumptions from the hearer. Using the term in the technical sense introduced in chapter 2, we are interested only in those assumptions that are *communicated* by an utterance.

But not all the assumptions communicated by an utterance are of interest to us here. My aim in this chapter is to try and explain why certain of the assumptions communicated by an utterance belong in a separate part of the book, or, in more technical terms, why we must distinguish between those assumptions that are *explicated* (explicitly communicated) by an utterance and those that are *implicated* (implicitly communicated).

This distinction does not correspond to any other distinctions that have been drawn by philosophers and linguists. In particular, it does not correspond to the distinction drawn by the philosopher Paul Grice (1989), between *saying* and *implicating*, a distinction which many would say lies at the heart of modern pragmatics. This is not to say that Grice's notion of an implicature has no contribution to make to pragmatics. On the contrary, in introducing this notion Grice was making a point of fundamental importance, namely, that understanding utterances is not simply a matter of knowing the meanings of the words uttered and the way in which they are combined. It also involves drawing inferences on the basis of non-linguistic information and the assumption that the speaker has aimed to meet certain general standards of communication. If there is dissatisfaction with Grice's proposals, it is because they don't go far enough. As Grice (and his followers) have recognized, non-linguistic information plays a role in disambiguation and reference assignment. However, what they have not appeared to notice is that the use of this non-linguistic information is governed by pragmatic principles – the same pragmatic principles which are needed for the recovery of implicatures.

Let us begin with the sort of example that Grice is interested in. In (1) speaker B doesn't actually *say* that he didn't enjoy his holiday. Nevertheless, this is what the hearer will derive from his answer.

(1)   A: Did you enjoy your holiday?
        B: The beaches were crowded and the hotel was full of bugs.

According to Grice, the answer 'No, I didn't enjoy my holiday' is an implicature recovered by the hearer on the basis of contextual information (crowded beaches and bugs are unpleasant) and the assumption that the speaker is providing a relevant answer to A's query. What the speaker says, on the other hand, is much more directly dependent on the meanings of the words B utters.

It would be a mistake to conclude, however, that pragmatic interpretation – that is, the use of contextual information and pragmatic principles – is involved only in the recovery of implicatures. As we have seen, the meanings of the words a speaker utters are frequently only a clue as to what he intends to convey. For example, we have been assuming in the discussion of (1) that the hearer takes the speaker to be referring to the beaches at his holiday resort and saying that they were crowded with other holiday-makers (rather than with jellyfish or seals). We have also been assuming that the hearer will take the speaker to have meant that his hotel was full of insects (rather than hidden microphones). Why? We cannot decide this solely by knowing the linguistic meanings of the words uttered.

According to the framework outlined in Part I, A's question gives the hearer access to a context in which the asssumption in (2) yields adequate contextual effects – in particular, it yields the implicature in (3).

(2)   The beaches at the holiday resort that the speaker went to were crowded with people and the hotel where he stayed was full of insects.
(3)   The speaker did not enjoy his holiday.

But why should the hearer assume that (2) is the proposition that the speaker intended to express? Surely there are other contexts which would enable the hearer to recover other propositions that yield contextual effects. Recall that the principle of relevance entitles the hearer to expect that she can obtain adequate contextual effects for no unjustifiable effort. In an ordinary conversation about holidays and hotels, the assumption that one's comfort can be affected by the presence of insects is rather more accessible than the assumption that microphones may have been hidden in one's room. Since this context yields adequate contextual effects, this interpretation is consistent with the principle of relevance. Moreover, the hearer is entitled to assume that this is the interpretation intended by the speaker, because a speaker who had intended to express some other proposition could have saved the hearer the effort of having first to consider (2) as a possible interpretation before going on to consider another. In other words, a speaker who was aiming at optimal relevance and who intended to express some other proposition should not have produced that utterance.

Someone might say here that since the recovery of (2) does involve inference, context and pragmatic principles, then it should be regarded as part of what is implicated rather than part of what is said. And indeed, this seems to be how some writers (notably Levinson (1987a, 1987c)) have interpreted Grice. If this is right, then I might as well stop writing this part of the book and go straight on to the next, for everything that I have taken to be part of what is explicated by an utterance, including the assignment of reference and disambiguation, would according to this criterion be part of what is implicated.

However, this does not seem to be what Grice intended.[1] More importantly, to define an implicature in this way is to ignore a fundamental difference between the way in which the hearer of B's utterance in (1) derives the assumption in (2) and the way in which she derives the assumption in (3). While (2) goes beyond the meanings of the words uttered, it is nevertheless directly dependent on those meanings in a way that (3) is not. The assumption in (2) is obtained by fleshing out a linguistically encoded semantic representation, in other words, by filling in the blueprint delivered by the grammar. The assumption in (3) is inferred from the fleshed-out semantic representation – that is, from the assumption in (2) – on the basis of contextual information and the presumption that the utterance is relevant. It is true that the process of fleshing out the semantic representation also involves the context and pragmatic principles. However, to say that (2) and (3) have the same status is to obscure the fact that (2), in contrast with (3), is derived by fleshing out the semantic representation of the utterance. Moreover, it obscures the fact that (3) is derived only once the hearer has derived (2), that is, the recovery of an implicature hinges on the hearer's understanding of what the speaker has said.

Sperber and Wilson (1986) call the result of fleshing out the semantic representation of an utterance an *explicature*. In some cases, for example in (4), the semantic representation provides only a very skeletal clue as to the explicature the hearer is intended to recover, and the process of developing the semantic representation into an explicature depends heavily on contextual information.

(4)   In there.

In other cases the speaker is more specific and the hearer's reliance on the context is less. Consider, for example, (5) and (6):

(5) It's in that room.
(6) The meeting is in room 307.

Though both utterances express the same proposition and hence have the same explicatures, there is a sense in which (6) is more explicit: there is less reliance on contextually inferred material. Just how explicit the speaker decides to be will, of course, depend on her assessment of the hearer's contextual resources.

In this part of the book, then, we are concerned with the way in which hearers use contextual information to flesh out or develop the semantic representation of an utterance. But into what? It might seem that the answer is simply that the hearer develops the semantic representation of an utterance into something with a truth value. The sentence that B uses in (1) cannot be said to be true or false, but it can be developed into something with a truth value by using contextual information to assign reference to the referring expressions and to disambiguate the ambiguous word *bug*.

However, the identification of the explicatures conveyed by an utterance cannot simply be a matter of obtaining a proposition that is truth evaluable. Consider the following examples (see Carston (1988b)):

(7) The park is some distance from my house.
(8) It will take us some time to get there.

The hearer of (7) could recover a complete (that is, truth-evaluable) proposition simply on the basis of the linguistic content of the utterance and reference assignment. This proposition would specify simply that the park and the house were not contiguous. However, this is surely not the proposition that the hearer would recover. This can be explained as follows. On the assumption that the speaker is not telling her something that is trivially true – that is, on the assumption that the speaker is being relevant – the hearer will use contextual information to recover a much more completely specified proposition, something like the one in (9).

(9) The park is further from my house than you might think.

This proposition, unlike the previous one, is not trivially true, and is likely to yield adequate contextual effects. A similar point can be made about the example in (8).

What these examples suggest is that the gap between linguistic meaning and the proposition expressed cannot be closed just by reference assignment and disambiguation, as Grice appears to have thought. In the next chapter we shall be looking at the processes involved in reference assignment in some detail. We shall also consider a number of phenomena which show how hearers *enrich* the semantic representation of an utterance in order to recover a proposition that is sufficiently relevant. In some cases, for example in the interpretation of ellipsed utterances like (4), the process of enrichment can be regarded as a matter of filling in gaps in a linguistically encoded semantic representation. In other cases the hearer's search for relevance leads her to enrich a semantic representation along lines that involve more than merely filling in gaps.

However, the process of enrichment is not confined to the recovery of the proposition expressed by an utterance. As we shall see in chapter 6, there are other propositions that the hearer can obtain by embedding the propositional content of the utterance into a higher-level description of the speaker's attitude towards the proposition he has expressed. For example, in producing the utterance in (10) the speaker may intend to communicate the higher-level descriptions in (11).

(10) I've got a lot of work to do.
(11) (a) The speaker believes that he has a lot of work to do.
     (b) The speaker regrets that he has a lot of work to do.

Indeed, the main relevance of the utterance may be understood to lie more in the speakers's attitude towards the proposition expressed than in the proposition itself.

Not all the higher-level descriptions recovered by a hearer are necessarily explicatures. The speaker of (10) may not have intended the hearer to notice that he was unhappy about the amount of work he had to do. The tone of regret in his voice may have been completely unintentional. Or he may have intended that the hearer notice his regret but not have intended that the hearer recognize that he intended her to notice this. However, our concern here is only with those cases in which the higher-level description has been overtly communicated, that is, we are concerned only with those higher-level descriptions that are explicated by an utterance.

The fact that a speaker wishes to convey a particular attitude towards the proposition he has expressed may or may not be evident from the linguistic form of his utterance. In some cases the hearer may be provided with a para-linguistic clue such as the speaker's tone of voice or the look on his face. In other cases the speaker may provide an explicit indication of the attitude he wishes to convey. Consider, for example, the role of the sentence adverbs in (12a) and (13a) and the performative verbs in (12b) and (13b):

(12) (a) Regrettably, I have a lot of work to do.
      (b) I regret that a have a lot of work to do.
(13) (a) Probably she will forget to come.
      (b) I predict that she will forget to come.

In many cases the linguistic form of the utterance provides only a clue to the attitude the speaker wishes to convey. For instance, indicative mood is usually associated with assertions. However, the speaker of (14) may be understood to be asking the hearer whether she is leaving or to be telling her to leave.

(14) You are leaving.

The interpretation recovered will depend on the context and the assumption that the utterance is optimally relevant.

Following Austin (1962) and Searle (1969), many writers see the role of mood and performative verbs in terms of their role in indicating the type of *speech act* the speaker is performing. That is, it is argued that language is used not to convey beliefs about the world but to perform actions, and that these actions must be described within a framework of social institutions. Thus, for example, the speaker of (15) is not describing a state of affairs or conveying his belief about a state of affairs. He is doing something which can be described only within a particular moral framework. And unless the hearer recognizes what the speaker is doing, communication will fail.

(15) I promise to end this chapter soon.

Similarly, the imperative mood of (16) is often seen as indicating that the hearer is expected to recognize that the speaker is issuing an order.

(16) Leave the cat alone.

Now, it might appear that this approach is able to handle a wider range of utterance types than the approach that we have been adopting. It is, after all, difficult to see how the imperative utterance in (16) could be analysed in terms of the communication of assumptions.

However, as we shall see in section 6.1, the speech-act framework of Austin and Searle is based on an assumption which cannot be maintained. The notion of a speech act, far from being fundamental to pragmatics, as some writers have claimed, is in fact of very limited use. It is true that the speaker of a non-declarative utterance like (16) does not communicate its propositional content as an explicature. What he communicates is a higher-level explicature which expresses his attitude towards that proposition.

As we shall see, speech-act theory has often been concerned with utterances that are in fact of no particular interest to pragmatics at all. At the same time, however, it has ignored a large class of utterances which are instances of communication, but which, like the imperative utterance in (16) do not communicate their propositional content. Although Romeo's utterance in (17) expresses the proposition that Juliet is the sun, one would not want to say that Romeo wished to communicate this proposition (as one of his beliefs).

(17)   Juliet is the sun.

We would, however, want to say that Romeo is communicating his thoughts about Juliet. What we need to explain, then, is the sense in which Romeo's utterance could be understood as a representation of his thoughts.

A similar problem arises with ironical utterances. If Jane has just arrived, as is her habit, half an hour late for a class, it is unlikely that the lecturer's utterance in (18) will be understood to be communicating the proposition it expresses.

(18)   It's nice to see you so bright and early again.

On the other hand, it is clear that the lecturer is communicating his attitude towards Jane's late arrival. Once again, this raises the question of how the speaker's attitude is communicated by his utterance.

The key to the interpretation of figurative utterances can be found in section 6.4, where Sperber and Wilson's notion of *interpretive use* is introduced. This notion can be used to explain a wide range of phenomena, including, as we shall see in section 6.6, the interpretation of interrrogative utterances. However, not all aspects of figurative meaning can be covered in this chapter, since they have more to do with implicature than with explicature.

Recommended Reading

The Explicature/Implicature Distinction

Sperber and Wilson 1986: 176–83.
Grice 1989: 87–8, 118–38.
Carston 1988b.
Recanati 1989.
Levinson 1989 (review of Sperber and Wilson 1986).

Speech Acts

See Recommended Reading for chapter 6.

Note

1 Grice himself pointed out that knowing what the speaker said in producing a particular utterance is a matter of, first, knowing what range of possible senses and possible referents could have been intended, and, second, knowing which sense and reference was intended on that occasion.

5   The Proposition Expressed

5.1   Assigning Reference

In the previous section we saw that the identification of explicatures includes both the recovery of the proposition expressed and the recovery of what we called higher-level explicatures. In this chapter we shall look in more detail at the way in which hearers recover the proposition expressed by an utterance. The account that emerges will not be a complete one. As we have seen, there are three subtasks involved in the recovery of the proposition expressed: reference assignment, disambiguation and enrichment. Here the discussion will be confined to just two of these subtasks: reference assignment and enrichment.

Referring Expressions

A referring expression is normally defined as an expression which on some occasion of utterance may be used to refer. But there are many ways in which a speaker may be said to refer, and, consequently, many different kinds of referring expressions. For example, a speaker may refer either to an individual (*singular reference*) or to a class of individuals (*general reference*). He may refer to some specific individual or class of individuals (*definite reference*) or he may not have a specific referent in mind (*indefinite reference*). In this section we shall be primarily concerned with what might be thought of as the basic kind of reference – singular definite reference. This means that we shall be concerned with the interpretation of definite descriptions (for example, the italicized phrases in (1a) and (1b)), proper names (illustrated in (1c)) and proforms (for example, the personal pronoun in (1d) and the demonstrative in (1e)):

(1)   (a)   *The plant* needed watering.
     (b)   I watered *your plant.*
     (c)   *Ben* watered your plant.

(d)   *He* is here.
(e)   *That* needs watering.

Of course, definite descriptions are not always used referentially. For example, the underlined noun phrase in (2) can be understood as having a predicative function.

(2)   Mr Lange is no longer *the prime minister of New Zealand*

As Donnellan (1966) pointed out, a definite noun phrase may be used non-referentially even when it is the subject of a sentence. For example, in (3) *Smith's murderer* might be used to refer to some specific individual – the man sitting there in the prison cell. However, there is another interpretation which may be paraphrased as in (4).

(3)   Smith's murderer must be insane.
(4)   Whoever murdered Smith must be insane.

Donnellan calls this non-referential use the attributive use. Obviously, the question of how the noun phrase is actually understood depends on the context and on pragmatic principles.

   Traditionally, the study of definite descriptions and proper names has been dominated by philosophical questions about existence and uniqueness,[1] while the study of pronouns has concentrated either on their role as *anaphors* or on their *deictic* or directly referential role. In its anaphoric use a pronoun is interpreted on the basis of the preceding linguistic or discourse context, whereas in its deictic use the referent is identified on the basis of the environment in which the utterance takes place. To illustrate this distinction, consider, first, the case in which you produce the utterance in (5) just after Ben has left the room.

(5)   *He* looked tired.

You may have nodded your head in Ben's direction, but there is no linguistic expression – that is, no antecedent – from which the pronoun picks up its interpretation. In contrast, in (6) *he* could be construed as being co-referential with the definite description *my uncle*.

(6)   My uncle came in. He looked tired.

Once an individual has been made salient a proform can be used for subsequent references. Indeed, it seems that subsequent references must be made by a pronoun. In (7a) the preferred interpretation is the one indicated by the indices, (7b) is unacceptable, and (7c) is acceptable only if *Tom* and *your brother* are not co-referential.

(7) (a) Tom^i is here. He^i has brought you a present.
    (b) Tom is here. ?? Tom has brought you a present.
    (c) Tom is here. Your brother has brought you a present.

At first it would seem that there are good reasons for treating proforms separately from names and definite descriptions, for it seems that in contrast with proforms, proper names and definite descriptions can be used only referentially. However, as Ariel (1988) points out, the situation is not as simple as this. On the one hand, both names and definite descriptions can be used anaphorically. Consider, for example, how you would interpret *the president* in (8).

(8) Ronald Reagan flew to Japan. The president is scheduled to meet with Japanese feminists. (example from Ariel 1988)

On the other hand, demonstratives, which, traditionally, are regarded as deictic, can be used anaphorically.

(9) Mrs Thatcher says she's not standing down. Honestly, *that woman* will never give up. (adapted from Ariel 1988)

These examples suggest that the difference between anaphoric and non-anaphoric referring expressions cannot be explained in purely linguistic terms. This is not, of course, to say that no difference exists. Later in the chapter we shall be looking at an approach to this distinction suggested by Kempson (forthcoming) which is based on the relevance-theoretic approach to pragmatics outlined in Part I. But first let us consider a more fundamental problem: what is it to assign reference to a referring expression?

Reference Assignment and Cognition

According to the approach adopted in formal semantics, reference assignment is simply a matter of locating an appropriate object. Although it is acknowledged that this depends on contextual factors, the context is often defined objectively, independently of the speaker or hearer. For instance, Lewis (1972) defines it as a set of co-ordinates, or times, individuals and places that supply the values for the variable expressions. According to Lewis, for the interpretation of (10) we would need an indicated object to supply the value of *this*, a place co-ordinate to supply the value of *here*, and a time co-ordinate to supply the value of *yesterday*:

(10)   This arrived yesterday.

We have already seen that this approach ignores the question of how the context is actually selected and therefore cannot specify anything more than a range of possible interpretations. This is not surprising. The problem of context selection could be addressed only by a theory which aimed to explain how hearers use their beliefs and assumptions in the interpretation of utterances, and the formal approach is concerned with language as an abstract system in which symbols are associated with the world rather than with the use of that system by any person. That is, this problem could be addressed only by a psychological theory of utterance interpretation.

Notice that when Lewis does address the question of context selection he is forced to acknowledge the role of mental factors in reference assignment.

> Consider the sentence 'The door is open'. This does not mean that the one and only door that now exists is open; nor does it mean that the one and only door near the place of utterance, or pointed at, is open. (1972: 214)

What the speaker means, says Lewis, is that the one and only door among the objects that are somehow prominent on the occasion of utterance is open. But contextual prominence is a subjective matter. Judgements about the salience of objects vary from person to person. As Lewis himself says, the interpretation of a definite description must depend on mental factors such as the hearer's expectations regarding the things the speaker is likely to bring to the attention of his audience.

However, although Lewis acknowledges the role of cognitive factors in reference assignment, his approach is non-cognitive in the sense that the result of assigning reference is still the location of an object. Contextual prominence or salience is a property of objects. As Wilson (1990) points out, this leaves him with the problem of explaining how we can talk about non-existent objects or events – for example, the book I would like to write or the seminar that was cancelled. It is not clear how these could be regarded as salient or prominent. On the other hand, it is clear that we can retrieve or construct mental representations of such objects/events. In other words, mental representations of non-existent objects or events may be highly accessible.

On a cognitive approach, reference assignment is not simply the identification of an appropriate object or event but, rather, involves accessing (that is, retrieving or constructing) a mental representation which uniquely identifies the intended referent. This representation is then incorporated into the proposition expressed by the utterance. For example, if in (11) the pronoun *it* is taken to refer to the book I want to write, then the propositional form of the utterance will be something like (12):

(11)   It is going to be a best seller.
(12)   The book Diane Blakemore is going to write is going to be a best seller.

On this approach, the question about reference assignment is not why a given referring expression identifies a particular individual but, rather, why a hearer presented with that referring expression accesses that mental representation. In other words, the question is why a hearer develops a given semantic representation involving a referring expression into a particular proposition. However, the examples in (7) suggest that not all referring expressions play the same role in the development of propositions, and, in particular, that whereas a name or definite description may be used to make a certain representation accessible, the use of a pronominal seems to assume the accessibility of a given representation.

Pronominals, Names and Definite Descriptions

According to Kempson (forthcoming), this difference derives from the fact that pronominals, in contrast with names and definite descriptions, do not have *nominal content*. As she shows, the significance of this difference lies in the relevance-theoretic assumptions which have been outlined in Part I of this book.[2]

To say that an expression has nominal content is to say that it is associated with a concept, and in particular that it is associated with a concept that gives the hearer access to certain encyclopaedic information. For example, the definite description *the ship* is associated with the concept *ship* which may have the following partial encyclopaedic entry:

(13)   Ship
            Ships float on water.
            Ships are large vessels.
            Ships may carry passengers.

And the name *Southampton* may be associated with the partial entry in (14).

(14)   Southampton
            Southampton is a port.
            Southampton is near Winchester.

Southampton is in Hampshire.
Southampton was bombed during the Second World War.

As we saw in chapter 1, such encyclopaedic information may become part of the context for the interpretation of the utterances which contains the expression in question, and, of course, for the interpretation of subsequent utterances. To take a simple example, in (15) the proper name *Southampton* may give the hearer access to information which enables her to derive the contextual implications in (16).

(15)   I live in Southampton.
(16)   (a)   Diane Blakemore lives near Winchester.
       (b)   Diane Blakemore lives in Hampshire.
       (c)   Diane Blakemore lives in a port.

Now since a proper name or definite description has nominal content, its use will give the hearer access to a context for the interpreted utterance which contains it. This means that it is possible to use a proper name or definite description to refer to an entity which has not necessarily been made salient either by the previous discourse or by the situation of the utterance. For example, as long as you do have a concept for *Tom* or *your brother* you will be able to recover a proposition from the utterances in (17a) and (17b) from which, using its encyclopaedic entry, you can derive contextual effects. That is, you should be able to derive a proposition that is sufficiently relevant:

(17)   (a)   Your brother is ill.
       (b)   Tom is ill.

In contrast, a pronominal has no nominal content and is not associated with a concept. What, for example, would the concept corresponding to *he* be? Consequently the use of a pronominal like *he* will not automatically give you access to contextual information which enables you to establish the relevance of the utterance. Instead, you must already *have* contextual information that has been made accessible either by previous discourse or by the situation of the utterance itself. According to this picture, pronominals play a very different role in utterance interpretation than do names and definite descriptions. Whereas names and definite descriptions encode concepts which simultaneously contribute to the content of the utterance and provide (through their encyclopaedic entries) access to contextual information which can be used in establishing relevance, pronominals are simply a key to a concept and a context which have their source either in the previous discourse or in the situation of utterance. Since this key has certain lexical properties – for example, *he* must refer to a male, *it* refers to an inanimate object – the hearer is constrained in her search for an appropriate concept and context. But as we have seen, such lexical clues are not always sufficient, and the hearer must make up the difference on the basis of pragmatic principles. The co-referential interpretation for *he* in (7a) cannot be stipulated by the grammar, but is, as Levinson (1987b) would say, a preferred interpretation.

The problem is to explain why this interpretation is preferred. However, before we address it we should remember that it is not restricted to pronominals like *he*. As we have seen, definite descriptions and names can be used anaphorically. Recall Ariel's example in (8) (repeated here):

(8) Ronald Reagan flew to Japan. The president is scheduled to meet with Japanese feminists.

The preferred interpretation for *the president* is one in which it is co-referential with *Ronald Reagan*. But this is not to say that *the president* functions as a pronominal. In particular, it is not to say that *the president* has no nominal content. Notice that while it is acceptable to use a definite description in the second segment of the sequence, a repetition of the name *Ronald Reagan* is unacceptable:

(18) Ronald Reagan flew to Japan. ?? Ronald Reagan is scheduled to meet with Japanese feminists.

The explanation for this is that a name and a definite description may differ in their conceptual content even though they may be used to pick out the same individual. This means that the use of the definite description can give the hearer access to contextual information not provided by the use of the name. And this means that the hearer may draw contextual implications from the second segment of (8) which she has not drawn from the first segment.

Accessibility and Relevance

According to the view being developed here, reference assignment involves the retrieval or construction of a mental representation which is incorporated into the proposition expressed. In some cases the speaker can trust the hearer to retrieve the required representation from memory. For instance, the speaker of the utterance in (19) may safely assume that I will access the representation associated with the noun phrase *your father* even though this representation has not been made accessible either through the previous discourse or by the situation itself.

(19)   Your father is here.

In other cases the representation must be made accessible either by the situation of utterance or by the preceding discourse. In the following dialogue the hearer's ability to supply the correct interpretation for *the oil* will depend on the interpretation of the preceding discourse or on her understanding of the situation in which the utterance was made. Are A and B making a salad or working on a car? And this interpretation provides an immediately accessible antecedent for the interpretation of *it*:

(20)   A: The oil is on the top shelf.
       B: Are you sure? I can't see it.

In many cases the situation of utterance or the preceding discourse may provide more than one accessible interpetation for a referring expression. For example, there may be two cupboards in the room where A and B are speaking and hence two possible referents for *the top shelf*. We have all been in the sort of situation where our understanding of an utterance leads us to look in the wrong place. As with all aspects of communication, referring involves a risk. What makes it a risk worth taking?

It might be tempting to think that much less risk is involved when the interpretation for a referring expression is made accessible by the immediately preceding discourse. Indeed, there are grammatical constraints on the interpretation of anaphora. For example, in (21) the embedded clause contains a zero noun phrase which must be construed with *Susan*:

(21)   Tom persuaded Susan [φ to go home].

However, the interpretation of anaphora cannot be solely a matter for the grammar. There is, for example, no linguistic reason why *it* should be co-referential with *the oil* in (20). This is only a preferred interpretation. [3]

But why is it preferred? Because of its accessibility? This suggests a psychological version of Lewis's (1972) salience principle: the preferred interpretation for a referring expression is the one that is most accessible. However, as Lewis himself recognized in a later paper (1979), accessibility (or salience) cannot be the only factor in reference assignment. He shows that in some cases the relative salience of objects has to be adjusted so that the result of reference assignment is pragmatically acceptable. One of his examples concerns two cats one of which (his) has just gained maximal salience over the course of the conversation. If the next utterance referring to a cat is unacceptable when this cat is chosen as the intended referent, then the hearer must assume that the other cat (yours) was intended to have maximal salience and hence be the one intended by the speaker. In other words, judgements about the comparative salience of potential referents must *accommodate* the assumption that the speaker is aiming to produce an acceptable utterance.

In contrast to his earlier (1972) account, Lewis's rule of accommodation captures a very important point about reference assignment: it depends on pragmatic principles. Unfortunately, however, Lewis does not give any satisfactory account of what these pragmatic principles might be. Moreover, the result of applying this rule is simply an adjustment to the salience ranking of possible referents. In a psychological account the search for pragmatic acceptability would lead the hearer to access a particular mental representation and incorporate it into the proposition expressed. In other words, in Lewis's example about the two cats, the hearer's search for pragmatic acceptability would lead her to recover a proposition about Lewis's cat rather than a proposition about your cat.[4]

But what is a pragmatically acceptable interpretation? According to the framework adopted in this book, it is the first interpretation consistent with the principle of relevance – that is, that a rational speaker aiming at optimal relevance might have intended. Let us return to the example in (20) which we shall now consider as part of the larger discourse in (22):

(22) B: I shall make the salad dressing.
     A: *The oil* is on the top shelf.
     B: Are you sure? I can't see *it*.

According to Sperber and Wilson, the hearer of A's utterance will make a hypothesis about the interpretation of *the oil*, and then test it for pragmatic acceptability (that is, consistency with the principle of relevance). If this hypothesis is pragmatically acceptable, then she will assume that this is the interpretation A intended.

Recall that according to this framework, the hearer starts out with an initial context consisting of the information she has most recently processed which can then be expanded in various ways. Let us assume that the most accessible information in B's entry for *salad dressing* is that given in (23):

(23) *salad dressing*
    The basic ingredient of salad dressing is some kind of vegetable oil.

Now suppose that in B's entry for *vegetable oil* the most accessible information is that given in (24):

(24) *vegetable oil*
    I do not know where A keeps his vegetable oil.

Given this information, together with his intention to make the salad dressing, it will be relevant for B to know where the oil is. In other words, the most accessible interpretation for *the oil* which yields adequate contextual effects is the vegetable oil that is required for making the salad dressing.

But why should B assume that this is the interpretation A intended? There are, after all, other possible contexts and hence other possible interpretations. Why doesn't B go on and test these hypotheses too?

Recall that a speaker aiming at optimal relevance must not only try to give the hearer adequate contextual effects, but also try to give these effects for the minimal necessary processing effort. That is, he must try to put the hearer to no unjustifiable effort in obtaining these effects. But a speaker who formulated his utterance in such a way that the most accessible interpretation which was pragmatically acceptable was not the one he intended *would* be putting the hearer to unjustifiable effort. Recovering and processing one interpretation involves less effort than recovering and testing two (or more) interpretations. This means that a hearer who finds that the most accessible interpretation is pragmatically acceptable does not have to go on to make and test other hypotheses. The first accessible interpretation which could rationally have been expected to yield adequate contextual effects for no unjustifiable effort is the only interpretation consistent with the principle of relevance.

As we have seen, the interpretation of *it* in (22) as co-referential with *the oil* is only a preferred interpretation. Now we can see that it is preferred on the grounds that it is the most accessible interpretation consistent with the principle of relevance. Notice that, textually speaking, it is not necessarily the most accessible interpretation: *the top shelf* might have some claim to be considered to be the most accessible antecedent. However, this is not the optimally relevant interpretation given B's question *Are you sure?* which will be interpreted as asking *Are you sure about the whereabouts of the oil?* In this context it is *the oil* which is the most accessible antecedent, and since its incorporation into the proposition expressed by B's utterance yields adequate contextual effects for no unjustifiable effort, it will be the interpretation which the hearer takes to have been intended by the speaker.

Bridging

In all the examples of anaphoric reference considered so far the antecedent is directly mentioned in the preceding text. For example, in (25) the hearer will assign reference to *he* by assuming that it is co-referential with *Nigel*.

(25)   Nigel arrived. He looked very pleased.

However, as H. Clark (1977) has shown, in many cases the interpretation of a referring expression has to be *bridged* by assumptions which are not directly mentioned in the preceding utterance, but which are constructed by a series of inferences on the basis of what the hearer knows or believes. For example, the first segment of (26) provides an antecedent for *the door* only by virtue of the assumption that fridges have doors.

(26)   Nigel bought a fridge. The door fell off three weeks later.

While fridges generally have doors, rooms do not generally have chandeliers. Nevertheless, a hearer will interpret *the chandeliers* in (27) as *the chandeliers in the room mentioned in the first segment*.

(27)   I walked into the room. The chandeliers sparkled brightly.

Similarly, although the fact that Tom went walking at noon does not entail that he walked in the park, the hearer of (28) will interpret *the park* as *the park where Tom walked*.

(28)   Tom went walking at noon. The park was beautiful.

Clark gives many more examples of this kind. In each case, he argues, the hearer has to construct an assumption which, since it is required for the assignment of reference, must be considered as an essential part of comprehension. Thus the assumption constructed by the hearer of (26) is given in (26′).

(26′)   The fridge had a door.

And the bridging assumptions constructed for the interpretation of (27) and (28) are (27′) and (28′) respectively.

(27′)The room had chandeliers.
(28′)Tom went walking in the park.

Notice that the hearer need not have had access to these assumptions prior to the utterance in question. It is not necessary, for example, to know beforehand that the room had chandeliers in order to interpret (27). The hearer would be able to access the hypothesis that the room had chandeliers from her contextual assumptions. On the assumption that the utterance is consistent with the principle of relevance, she would then take it that she is to upgrade this hypothesis to an assumption whose truth is guaranteed by the speaker. In other words, the assumptions in (26′), (27′) and (28′) are what we shall be calling *implicated assumptions*.[5] However, in contrast to the implicated assumptions we shall be discussing in Part III, the role of these assumptions is not to yield contextual implications, but to establish the referential content of the utterance. That is, their role is to help with the identification of the explicatures conveyed by the utterance. Hence their appearance in this part of the book rather than the next.

The implicated assumption in (26′) plays a role in the identification of the referential content of the second segment of (26) by giving the hearer access to an antecedent for *the door*. In terms of the approach being adopted here, this means that the hearer incorporates the mental representation made accessible by (26′) into the propositional content of the utterance. Using indexing we could represent the propositional content of this utterance thus:[6]

(29)   Nigel bought a fridge$_i$. The door of the fridge$_i$ fell off three weeks later.[7]

But why is the correct bridge the one that links *the door* to the door of the fridge that Nigel bought and not, say, a bridge that links *the door* to the door of the speaker's house? According to Clark, the best bridge is the shortest one that is consistent with a pragmatic criterion he calls the Given–New Contract. This criterion requires the speaker to ensure that the referent of a referring expression is uniquely identifiable from memory (that is, given) and then to say something new about that referent.[8]

However, there may be more than one accessible bridge. Consider, for example, the sequence in (30).

(30)   Nigel bought a fridge and put it in the caravan. Three weeks later the door fell off.

As we have seen, the hearer should be able to access the hypothesis that the fridge had a door from her encyclopaedic knowledge. But equally, she should be able to access the hypothesis that the caravan had a door. Which bridge should she use? It seems that most hearers would interpret *the door* in (30) as the door of the fridge rather than as the door of the caravan. Why?

Recall that the hearer's aim in the assignment of reference is to construct a proposition which is optimally relevant in a way that the speaker could have manifestly foreseen. There might well be a context in which it would be relevant that the door of Nigel's caravan fell off. However, given the assumptions about what people expect when they buy something, it is easier, on the basis of what has gone before, to construct a context in which it would be relevant to know that the door of the fridge that Nigel had just bought fell off. In other words, as with the interpretation of anaphoric expressions, the assignment of reference depends not just on the accessibility of the referent, but also on the accessibility of a context in which the proposition expressed by the speaker is relevant.

Exercise 1

Discuss the way in which the interpretation of the first segment of the following helps with the identification of the proposition expressed by the second.

> The last of the allied prisoners of war have been flown to Saudi Arabia. There were thirty five on board, including nine Britons. (from a radio news broadcast)

5.2 Enrichment

That the linguistic properties of an utterance may provide only very skeletal clues as to the proposition the hearer is intended to construct is familiar from such highly elliptical utterances as B's response in (31).

(31) A: Where did you put the money?
     B: Under the mattress.

In normal circumstances the hearer will be able to use these clues to construct the complete proposition in (32).

(32) B put the money under the mattress.

The problem for a theory of utterance interpretation is to explain why the hearer constructs this proposition and not, say, the one in (33).

(33) B found a copy of *Syntactic Structures* under the mattress.

In some cases it might seem that the process of interpreting the linguistic clues is a matter of filling in the slots left open in the linguistically encoded semantic representation. For example, in (31) the hearer is expected to supply whatever is needed to complete a verb phrase, and then to supply a subject noun phrase to complete the sentence. However, in this section we shall see that the problem of explaining how the hearer arrives at a complete proposition is not confined to these familiar cases of ellipsis, but extends to cases in which the grammar does not provide any empty slots. As we shall see, these cases have been studied by other writers (for example, Levinson (1987a, b, c) and Horn (1983, 1988)) under the heading of *generalized conversational implicature*.[9] This means that their inclusion in this part of the book raises the controversial questions about the distinction between explicature and implicature discussed in chapter 4.

Conjoined Utterances

According to logicians, the meaning of *&* is given in the truth-table in (34).

(34)

P	&	Q
t	t	t
t	f	f
f	f	t
f	f	f

What this says is that *&* forms a conjoined proposition *P & Q* which is true if and only if both its conjuncts are true. In other words, *&* is *truth-functional*. The truth of a conjoined proposition can be predicted entirely on the basis of the truth values of its conjuncts. Thus if we agree that the first conjunct of (35) is false, then we have to say that the whole conjoined proposition is false.

(35) Paris is the capital city of Italy and Wellington is the capital city of New Zealand.

Not all connectives are truth-functional. Consider, for example, the natural language connective *because*. In (36) the truth of the conjunction cannot be predicted on the basis of the truth of its conjuncts.

(36) Nigel left because the band started playing.

It could be, for example, that Nigel left and the band started playing, but that neither event caused the other.

My main concern here, however, is with the question of whether what logicians have said about *&* applies to the natural language counterpart *and*: that is, with whether *and* in natural language is truth-functional.

The problem is well known. There are utterances containing *and* which seem to convey more than the truth of their conjuncts. While the logician's definition of *&* might carry over to *and* in the example in (35), it does not seem to apply in the case of (37) or (38):

(37)   Jane got on her bike and rode down the path.
(38)   The road was icy and he slipped.

In (37) there is a suggestion that Jane rode down the path after she had got on her bike, while in (38) there is a suggestion that his slipping is a result of the icy state of the road. The question is whether these temporal and causal connotations are part of the meaning of *and*, or, in other words, whether *and* is ambiguous between *&*, *and then*, and *and because of that*.

There is plenty of evidence against this lexical-ambiguity analysis. First, genuine lexical ambiguity is typically language-specific: *duck* is ambiguous in a way that the French equivalent *canard* is not. The connotations carried by conjoined utterances, on the other hand, seem to be carried in all languages.

Second, as Grice (1975, 1989) pointed out, these suggestions can be cancelled without contradiction. Whereas it is impossible to produce the utterance in (36) and then go on to say, 'But there was no connection', it is possible to utter (38) and then to deny a causal connection. This suggests that the connotations are not linguistically determined but depend on the context.

Third, another point made by Grice, the connotations arise even when *and* is replaced by a pause or fullstop (period). For example, the fact that (39) conveys the same temporal connotation as (37) suggests that this is a discourse phenomenon rather than a lexical one.

(39)   Jane got on her bike. She rode down the path.

Finally, as Posner (1980) has pointed out, the suggestions conveyed by conjoined utterances are not restricted to the temporal and causal ones illustrated in (37) and (38). If we say that these connotations are due to the meaning of *and*, then we are going to have to say the same thing about the suggestions conveyed in the following examples (adapted from Posner 1980: 187):

(40)   (a)   Simon was in the kitchen and he was making bread.   (... *and there* ...)
       (b)   Jane fell into a deep sleep and dreamed she was a sea-gull.   (... *and during this time* ...)
       (c)   The window was open and there was a draught.   (... *and coming from it* ...)

If *and* is ambiguous, then it is multiply ambiguous. If true, this is puzzling in itself, and would not explain why the same 'ambiguities' arise in non-conjoined sequences. It seems more plausible that the explanation for these phenomena lies in pragmatics than in lexical semantics.

Grice himself provided a pragmatic account of the temporal connotations of conjoined utterances in terms of his Manner maxim, and, in particular, the sub-maxim 'Be orderly':

> if what one is engaged upon is a narrative (if one is talking about events), then the most orderly manner for a narration of events is an order that corresponds to the order in which they took place. So the meaning of the expression 'He took off his trousers and got into bed' and the corresponding expression with a logician's constant *&* (i.e. 'he took off his trousers & he got into bed') would be exactly the same. (Grice 1981: 186)

Clearly, the Manner maxim is not going to help us explain the suggestions in (40). Nevertheless, Grice has established a strong case for a pragmatic explanation of the interpretation of conjoined utterances.

For Grice, and many of his followers (for example, Gazdar (1979), Horn (1972), Levinson (1987a)), this meant that the suggestions conveyed by conjoined utterances are implicatures. However, as Cohen (1971) has shown, there are examples which show that they must be treated as part of the proposition expressed. Consider (41) and (42):

(41)   If the old king has died of a heart attack and a republic has been declared, then Sam will be happy, but if a republic has been declared and the old king has died of a heart attack, then Sam will be unhappy. (adapted from Cohen (1971))

(42)   It's always the same at parties: either you get drunk and no one will talk to you or no one will talk to you and you get drunk. (example from D. Wilson)

If the temporal connotations are implicatures, then a sentence of the form P and Q should be equivalent to one of the form Q and P. But with (41) and (42) this is not the case: (41) is not contradictory, and (42) is not just a redundant repetition.

Cohen takes this to be evidence against the implicature account in favour of the lexical ambiguity account in which *and* means *and then* and *and because of that* in addition to its truth-functional sense. However, while such examples may be evidence against the implicature account, they are not necessarily counter-examples to a pragmatic account. Indeed, Carston (1988b) has shown that these examples can be regarded as evidence for an analysis in which these suggestions are pragmatically determined aspects of the proposition expressed.

According to the view adopted in this book, implicatures are assumptions derived from the proposition that the hearer takes the speaker to have expressed together with the context. But the hearer cannot identify the proposition that has been expressed without taking account of the context either. In order to recover a proposition that is truth-evaluable the speaker must assign reference to referring expressions and disambiguate ambiguous expressions. And this, as we have seen, depends on the context. But the hearer's aim cannot be simply to recover a proposition that is truth-evaluable. Recall the example discussed in chapter 4, repeated here:

(43)   The park is some distance from my house.

As we saw, on the basis of the linguistic meaning of the utterance and reference assignment the hearer of (43) would be able to recover only a trivially true proposition. On the assumption that the speaker is presenting information which yields adequate contextual effects, the hearer will recover a much more completely specified proposition, one along the lines of (44):

(44)   The park is further from my house than you might think.

A similar point is made by the contrast between (45) and (46) (examples adapted from Sperber and Wilson).

(45)   I've had breakfast.
(46)   I've been to New Zealand.

While the hearer will take the speaker of (46) to mean that he had been to New Zealand at some point in his life, it is most unlikely that she will take the speaker of (45) to mean that he had had breakfast at some point in his life. Why?

Although it may be true that the speaker had had breakfast at some point in his life, this would not normally be sufficiently relevant to merit the hearer's attention. The hearer will assume that the speaker has produced an utterance that is worthy of her attention. That is, she will assume that the speaker has been relevant. Accordingly, she will generally construe the speaker as expressing the proposition in (47).

(47)   The speaker has had breakfast today.

There is a sense in which this proposition contains more than what the speaker actually said. However, there is no sense in which (47) is a conclusion derived from what the speaker actually said. Like all explicatures, (47) is a development of the linguistically encoded semantic representation of the utterance. More particularly, it is the result of enriching this semantic representation in accordance with the hearer's aim of recovering an interpretation consistent with the principle of relevance.

In applying these ideas to the analysis of conjoined utterances Carston makes the quite standard assumption that an utterance describing an event is interpreted as expressing a value for a time index determined on the basis of the context. Her point is that, given her background beliefs and the principle of relevance, the hearer can go beyond the linguistically encoded meaning of an utterance like (37) (repeated below) and recover values for the time index in each conjunct so that if the value of the index in the first conjunct is t, the value for the index in the second conjunct is $t + n$. The proposition recovered is represented as (48):

(37)   Jane got on her bike and rode down the path.
(48) $Jane_i$ got on her bike at t and she_i rode down the path at $t + n$

More generally, the optimally relevant interpretation of a conjoined utterance may go beyond its linguistically encoded content so that its second conjunct includes information determined by the interpretation of the first. This allows us to account for a wide range of suggestions, including the suggestion not mentioned in our earlier discussion of (37) that Jane rode down the path on her bike. Let us see how it allows us to account for the causal connotations of utterances like (39) (repeated here).

(38)   The road was icy and he slipped.

That an event occurred does not entail that it had a cause. Nevertheless, the optimally relevant interpretation of a conjoined utterance may be one whose second conjunct is enriched by the inclusion of a causal predicate whose argument is determined by the interpretation of the first conjunct. Thus the hearer of (38) may recover the proposition in (49).

(49) $[The road was icy]_i$ and because of $that_i$ he slipped.

According to the account just given, the causal and temporal connotations of conjoined utterances are examples of the connections that characterize any coherent discourse. That is, they arise from the way that information made available by the interpretation of one discourse segment is used in establishing the proposition expressed by the next. It is not surprising, then, that these suggestions can be conveyed either by conjoined utterances or by non-conjoined discourse sequences like (39) (repeated here).[10]

(39)   Jane got on her bike. She rode down the path.

In the next section we will look at the connectivity of discourse in more detail. However, let us conclude this section with an exercise which illustrates a further aspect of enrichment.

Exercise 2

Discuss the interpretation of the italicised genitive noun phrases in the following from the point of view of the pragmatic enrichment of linguistic form. How would you characterize the meaning of the genitive?

(a)   I have borrowed *Jane's car*.
(b)   I would hate to have *Simon's job*.
(c)   Can I borrow *your copy of 'Barriers'*?
(d)   Should I read *your book*?
(e)   That was Alfred Brendel playing the first of *his two concertos* tonight.
(f)   Hurry up. *Your programme* is on.
(g)   Oh no. You've made dirty marks all over *my nice clean floor*.
(h)   I'm going to be late for *my class*.
(i)   *Yesterday's events* really shocked *the country's president*.
(j)   *The train's arrival* was accompanied by a large explosion.
(k)   *The city's destruction* was deplored by the government.
(l)   *Jane's father* has bought her a car.

Bibliographical note: For a discussion of the view that the possessive construction is semantically indeterminate see Kempson (1977: 125). Taylor (1989) argues that although many possessive expressions would seem at first sight to have little to do with possession in the strict sense, the relation of possession has a privileged status in the semantics of such constructions so that the central use of the possessive construction is to identify an entity in terms of its possession by another entity. However, note that Taylor defines possession in very broad terms.

5.3 Explicatures and Coherence

This chapter has had two major objectives: First, it has aimed to show that the proposition expressed by an utterance depends on the contextual information that the hearer brings to bear on its interpretation. Second, it has aimed to show that the mere accessibility of contextual information is not enough to guarantee its use in the recovery of the proposition expressed, and that the interpretation recovered must be constrained by pragmatic principles. In the majority of the cases we have considered, the contextual information used in the identification of the proposition expressed is made available through the interpretation of the preceding discourse. In the case of anaphoric expressions this role was quite direct, while in the case of bridging cross-reference and conjoined utterances we saw that the preceding discourse may play a more indirect role in providing access to contextual information which is used for making inferences.

However, the role of the context is not restricted to the interpretation of utterances that are part of a discourse or text. We have already seen that referring expressions can be used non-anaphorically. Moreover, the processes of enrichment described in section 5.2 are also involved in the interpretation of isolated utterances. This section addresses the question of whether the pragmatic principles which constrain the use of contextual information in the interpretation of utterances that are part of discourse are different from the principles that constrain its use in the interpretation of isolated utterances.

It is clear that a planned discourse is not simply an arbitrary sequence of utterances. It is very difficult, for example, to see how the following would be regarded as a planned discourse.

(50) The committee met at two o'clock last Thursday. Now is the time to plant your spring bulbs. I never read the local newspaper. These days most writers use word processors. It is very likely that the prime minister will resign.

This has led many writers to try to uncover the source of the connectivity of discourse. Some, for example Halliday and Hasan (1976), are concerned primarily with the linguistic devices for creating connectivity – that is, *cohesion*:

> Cohesion is part of the system of language. The potential for cohesion lies in the systematic resources of reference, ellipsis, and so on that are built into the language itself. (1976: 5)

For example, the anaphoric relationship between the pronoun *it* and the noun phrase *the oil* in (20) (repeated here as (51)) contributes to what Halliday and Hasan call the *texture* of the dialogue.

(51) A: The oil is on the top shelf.
      B: Are you sure? I can't see it.

In (52) the use of *so* contributes towards textual cohesion by indicating a particular kind of connection between the two conjuncts, while in (53) the use of *then* specifies a different kind of connection:

(52) He was tired and so he went to bed.
(53) He wrote a letter and then went to bed.

However, meaning relations do not have to be realized explicitly for a discourse to have coherence. As we saw in the last section, both the causal connection in (52) and the temporal connection in (53) could have been conveyed implicitly:

(54) He was tired and he went to bed.
(55) He wrote a letter and went to bed.

Moreover, even when two sentences are related by a cohesive tie, the hearer has to go beyond her linguistic resources to recover an interpretation. For example, in (56) (adapted from Hobbs (1979)) *he* could in principle refer to either John or Bill:

(56) John can open Bill's safe. He knows the combination.

This would seem to suggest that we need to move from linguistic connectivity to connectivity of content. Hobbs (1978), for example, argues that the coherence of a text or discourse can be defined in terms of a set of structural binary relations between its segments, which depend on their propositional content. A speaker who wishes to be understood must ensure that his utterance stands in one of these relations to the preceding text, and a hearer who wishes to understand the utterance must recognize which particular relation it bears to the preceding text. In other words, we have a menu of discourse connec- tions, the speaker's task being to select a connection and the hearer's task being to identify the speaker's choice. For example, one of the items on Hobbs' menu is the relation of *elaboration* which subsumes 'trivial' moves like pure repetitions, repairs and tag questions as well as those cases in which the speaker conveys 'the same message from two different perspectives' (1978:

25). It is the recognition of this relation, claims Hobbs, that accounts for the hearer's interpretation of *he* in (56) above as co-referential with John rather than Bill.

Exercise 3

Discuss the problems that the following sequence presents for Hobbs' view that the coherence of a text can be defined in terms of a set of structural binary relations.

> John was late. The eight o'clock news was virtually over. The situation in the Gulf had not changed. The threat of war had an enormous effect on petrol prices. Susan could no longer afford to drive to work. At least all that walking was making her fit. She would now be able to go on the expedition the Swiss Alps. It was being organized by the university. The university cannot afford to run many trips of this kind. The education cuts have necessitated a big cut in spending. The Arts Faculty has no money for new computers this year.

Note: See van Dijk (1977: 130–55) for one approach to this problem. See Blakemore (1988) and Blass (1990: 25–7) for a critique of this approach.

Now it is evident that hearers are able to identify specific connections which, as Halliday and Hasan have recognized, may be coded in the language. Equally, however, it is evident that a speaker cannot use just any coherence relation in order to continue the discourse. Moreover, as Blass (1990: 17–20) shows, a text appropriate in one context may be inappropriate in another. For example, the second segment of (57) could be understood as an elaboration of the second, but while it may be appropriate as part of an autobiography, it would not be appropriate as part of a *curriculum vitae*.

(57) I was born in Lower Hutt, New Zealand. It used to be a dormitory suburb of Wellington, but is now a busy town with high-rise office blocks. (adapted from Blass 1990: 19)

This suggests that a theory of discourse organization cannot consist simply of a taxonomy of coherence relations. It must also include the principles that constrain the speaker's choice of utterance, or, in other words, an account of the acceptability of utterances in discourse.

For some writers pragmatic acceptability means coherence, or as van Dijk (1977: 1–13) calls it, 'textual structure':

> Those utterances which can be assigned textual structure are thus acceptable discourses of the language – at this level of the account of acceptability, i.e. are well-formed and interpretable. (1977: 3)

But as Sperber and Wilson (1985) have pointed out, the pragmatically acceptable interpretation of a segment of discourse is not always the coherent one. Consider the dialogue in (58) (adapted from Blass 1990: 73):

(58) A: What did Jane say?
      B: The bus is coming.

B's response can be construed either as a report of an assertion made by Jane or as an assertion by B that the bus is coming. According to the coherence-based approach, only the first interpretation should be possible, and the referring expression *the bus* would be interpreted accordingly. But of course, it is not difficult to imagine circumstances in which the other (non-coherent) interpretation would be recovered and *the bus* would be taken to refer to the bus that A and B are waiting for.

It may be objected here that this is a case of unplanned discourse, and is therefore subject to entirely different kinds of constraints than the examples discussed in the coherence literature. But a theory which was restricted to the interpretation of utterances in planned discourse would not only be committed to ignoring a very large proportion of human discourse, but would also have nothing to say about the interpretation of isolated utterances. Moreover, as Deirdre Wilson (personal communication) has pointed out, planned texts themselves reproduce unplanned discourse (for example, dialogues in novels). So even an account of planned texts would have to deal with unplanned texts.

The fact that an utterance does not follow on from the preceding discourse or is not part of a discourse at all does not mean that it can be understood in isolation from the context. And while it is true that planned discourse is characterized by a kind of coherence not found in unplanned discourse, the principles which constrain the selection and use of contextual information in the interpretation of an utterance that is part of a planned discourse need not necessarily be different from the ones that govern its selection and use in the interpretation of an isolated utterance or an utterance that is part of an unplanned discourse.

It should be recalled here that by *context* we mean the beliefs and assumptions the hearer constructs for the interpretation of an utterance either on the basis of her perceptual abilities or on the basis of the assumptions she has stored in memory or on the basis of her interpretation of previous utterances. That is, we have defined the context in psychological terms, and the psychological processes involved in using the context in interpretation are the same whatever its source. Equally, the principles constraining those processes do not vary according to whether the context is derived through the interpretation of a preceding utterance or not.

At the same time, however, this approach provides a very good reason why the assumptions derived from the interpretation of one utterance can be used as context for the interpretation of the next. Recall that the hearer's aim is to minimize processing costs. This means she will aim to process newly presented information in the smallest, most accessible context available. Such a context is provided by the interpretation of the immediately preceding utterance (or utterances). But this context may not necessarily yield adequate contextual effects. Hence the possibility of the non-coherent interpretation in utterances such as (60B).

However, as we have seen, the interpretation of an utterance is not restricted to the identification of the proposition expressed. It also includes assumptions which are implicitly communicated. Since the contextual information used in the recovery of such assumptions may be made available through the interpretation of preceding discourse, we would expect that the coherence of discourse may also derive from the fact that the interpretation of one segment gives the hearer access to a context which enables her to derive assumptions that are implicated by the next. An examination of this aspect of coherence will have to wait until the chapters on implicature in Part III. However, while we might have finished with the identification of the proposition expressed, we have not yet finished with explicature. Let us now turn to the identification of what we have called *higher—level explicatures*.

Recommended Reading

Reference

Relevance Theory
Sperber and Wilson 1986: 183–4, 190–4, 204–8.
Wilson (forthcoming).

A general introduction to reference and referring terms
Lyons 1977 vol. 1: 174–7; vol. 2: 636–77.

Philosophical papers on definite descriptions and proper names
See papers in Steinberg and Jakobovits 1971: 76–142.

Formal semantics approaches
Lewis 1972, 1979.

Pragmatic approaches to anaphora
Ariel 1988; 1990: chs 0–3.
Kempson 1985.
Levinson 1987b (an implicature account).

Bridging
H. Clark 1977.
Sperber and Wilson 1986 (relevance-theoretic approach).

Enrichment

Relevance Theory
Sperber and Wilson 1986: 181, 183–4, 188–91, 204.
Carston 1988b, 1990.

Grice on conjunction
Grice 1981; 1989: 68, 70, 201.
Cohen 1971 (critique of Grice).
Posner 1980 (critique of Grice).

Generalized implicature approach
Levinson 1987a.

Coherence

Relevance Theory
Sperber and Wilson 1986: 263 n.19.
Blass 1990: chs 1–2.

Coherence and discourse analysis
G. Brown and Yule 1983: chs 6–7.

Text grammar approaches
van Dijk 1977.

Cohesion and linguistic structure
Halliday and Hasan 1976: see especially ch. 1.

Notes

1 See, for example, Frege (1892), Russell (1919) and Strawson (1956).
2 The following account is a considerably edited version of Kempson's explanation, and, needless to say, I do not hold her responsible for any errors.

3 Recently, a number of writers have demonstrated that the interpretation of anaphors may be even less a matter for the grammar than is normally thought. See, for example, Reinhart (1983), Ariel (1988, 1990), Levinson (1987b) and Kempson (1985, forthcoming). For a critique of these pragmatic approaches see Kleiber (1990).

4 This is a very rough characterization of the propositional content recovered. I do not wish to suggest that the propositional content of an utterance might contain indexical expressions like *your cat*. There are various possibilities as to what the propositional representation might look like. For example, we might use indexing – *the cat owned by* X (where X is your name). Or, as Deirdre Wilson (personal communication) has suggested to me, the hearer might construct a proper name, *the cat E26 owned by E59*.

5 See chapter 7 for a more detailed examination of implicated assumptions.

6 But see n. 4.

7 In fact, this is not how Clark analyses the interpretation of these utterances. He suggests that the assumption the hearer constructs is something like

> The fridge mentioned had a door.
> This is the antecedent for *the door*.

That is, whereas Sperber and Wilson's account involves both implicature and explicature, Clark's account involves only implicature.

8 Wilson (1990) has shown that it is not true that a unique bridge is required. For example, the hearer of the following sentence will understand *the door* to mean the door of the hearer's car, but will not necessarily know which door (front, back, passenger, driver) was intended.

> I can't drive my car. The door needs mending.

It does not matter, of course. The utterance will be optimally relevant whichever door it is.

9 This notion was introduced by Grice (1975, 1989).

10 However, there are examples which suggest that there are connotations conveyed by non-conjoined sequences that cannot be conveyed by conjoined utterances. In the following example noted by H. Clark (cited by Gazdar 1979: 4) there is a suggestion that the iciness of the road is an explanation for his slipping:

> He slipped. The road was icy.

As Gazdar points out, this suggestion cannot be conveyed by the corresponding conjoined utterance:

> He slipped and the road was icy.

Bar-Lev and Palacas (1980) also discuss a range of examples in which the connotations carried by non-conjoined sequences are not carried by the corresponding conjoined ones. See Blakemore (1987: 113–25) for a suggestion as to how this discrepancy might be explained in relevance-theoretic terms. Also see Wilson (1990) for further discussion.

6 Higher-Level Explicatures: Attitudes and Speech Acts

6.1 Speech Acts and Pragmatics

So far in this part of the book we have restricted our attention to utterances in which the proposition expressed describes a state of affairs. Thus for example, the utterance in (1) expresses a proposition which describes a state of affairs in which there is a snake in the grass.

(1) There's a snake in the grass.

This restrictiveness is not surprising given that our examples have all been declarative sentences. Utterances of imperative sentences like (2), interrogative sentences like (3), and exclamatives like (4) could hardly be interpreted as expressing a proposition which was relevant as a description of the world:

(2) Put it in the sack.
(3) Is it poisonous?
(4) What a beautiful colour.

But even the interpretation of utterances with declarative form like (1) cannot be discussed simply in terms of the recovery of a proposition which is a description of a state of affairs. The speaker of (1) could be guessing that there is a snake, he could be claiming that there is a snake, or he could be warning the hearer that there is a snake. He could be expressing his surprise that there is a snake, or his relief that there is a snake. Whatever he is doing he could not be described simply as expressing the proposition that there is a snake is the grass.

The fact that language is not used just to describe the world was the starting-point for Austin's (1962) theory of speech acts. He pointed out that language can be used to create obligations (consider (5)), to influence the actions of others (consider (6)), and to create new social relationships (consider (7)).

(5)   I promise that I will not smoke.
(6)   Stop smoking.
(7)   I pronounce you man and wife

More generally, language can be used not just for describing existing states of affairs, but also for creating new ones.

If this is so, then we must no longer speak of the thoughts and beliefs conveyed by utterances, but rather of the acts speakers perform, or of the *illocutionary forces* of utterances. Moreover, a theory of language use will have to specify what types of acts can be performed by speakers and the conditions under which a particular kind of act is successful. This is essentially Searle's project in his (1969) *Speech Acts*.[1]

The assumption underlying this project is that the classification of speech acts plays an essential role in communication, so that what is communicated by an utterance is that it belongs to a particular speech-act type (or has a particular illocutionary force). For example, a speaker who wishes to issue a warning must communicate that he is issuing a warning, a speaker who is making a guess must communicate that he is making a guess, and a speaker who is making a promise must communicate that he is making a promise. And in each case the hearer will understand the utterance only if she can identify the type of speech-act being performed. That is, according to speech-act theory, communication is not just a matter of having your intentions recognized. It is, more specifically, a matter of having your intention to perform a particular type of speech act recognized.

Is this assumption justified? First, let us see that in the case of many so-called speech acts it is not even necessary to have an audience who is capable of recognizing your intentions. Naming ships, baptizing babies and consecrating buildings all happen to involve language. At the same time, however, they can be successfully performed in the presence of an uncomprehending audience or in the presence of no audience at all. These 'speech acts' do not really have to have anything to do with communication, and hence pragmatics, at all.

Now, let us consider speech acts like betting and promising. A speaker who intended to make a bet would not succeed if he communicated just the proposition in (8).

(8)   Jane will leave the room.

The hearer would only ask 'How much?' if she understands the speaker to be also communicating the proposition in (9).

(9)   The speaker is betting that Jane will leave the room.

Similarly, a speaker who communicated only the proposition in (10) would not be open to moral retribution should he decide to smoke.

(10) The speaker will not smoke.

Retribution would be in order only if he had also communicated the proposition in (11).

(11) The speaker is promising that he will not smoke.

In other words, a hearer who did not recover (11) from an utterance would miss out on some of its intended relevance. These cases, then, do conform to the speech-act theory of communication: the hearer's understanding of the utterance depends on her having recognized that a certain type of speech act is being performed. As Sperber and Wilson put it, betting and promising are *communicated acts*.

It is easy to see that this is a consequence of the fact that betting and promising can be described only with reference to a particular social framework or institution. Because, for example, promising exists only given a moral framework in which people can put themselves under a particular kind of moral obligation (a kind different from that involved in, say, swearing), a hearer who did not see that a promise was being made would miss out on the intended relevance of an utterance meant as a promise.

But this does not mean that a theory of pragmatics must include a theory of social institutions. As Sperber and Wilson say, we must distinguish what goes on at the institutional level and what goes on at the communicative level. That some institutional knowledge is involved in the interpretation of bets and promises is, as they put it, 'no more and no less interesting to pragmatics than the fact that in order to discover by looking out of the window that there is rain on the way some meteorological knowledge is required' (1985: 12).

In contrast with these cases, there are many so-called speech acts whose successful performance does not depend on the hearer's ability to recover a description of the speaker's intentions. Consider, for example, what is involved in understanding the utterance in (12) as a warning.

(12) The path is slippery here.

According to the speech-act view, a speaker who intends (12) as a warning must intend the hearer to recover the proposition in (13).

(13) The speaker of (12) is warning the hearer that the path is slippery here.

But surely this is not necessarily the case. A speaker who intends (12) to be interpreted as a warning simply intends the hearer to interpret the utterance in a particular way. More specifically, he intends the hearer to make certain sorts of inferences – ones that have to do with the unpleasant or dangerous consequences of the state of affairs the utterance describes. Obviously, this is not the only possible interpretation for the utterance in (12). The speaker and hearer might have been deciding which parts of the path need anti-slime treatment. If she does recover such an interpretation, it is because this is the optimally relevant interpretation, given the contextual assumptions she has available and not because she has recovered the proposition in (13). If she does identify the speaker's intentions in this way, it is because she has already understood the relevance of the utterance. In other words, the main relevance of the utterance lies in the proposition that the path is slippery in the place indicated.

The same kind of point can be made about a whole range of so-called assertive speech acts. For example, that the speaker of (14) intends his utterance to be understood as a guess rather than as a claim does not mean that he expects the hearer to recover (15) rather than (16) as a description of his intentions.

(14)   It's an owl.
(15)   The speaker of (14) is guessing that it is an owl.
(16)   The speaker of (14) is claiming that it is an owl.

To intend an utterance as a guess is to intend that the hearer recognize that the speaker does not have conclusive evidence for the truth of the proposition expressed, and hence that he cannot be taken to be strongly committed to its factuality. In other words, understanding an utterance as a guess is not so much a matter of recovering a description of the speaker's intention to perform a particular type of speech act as it is a matter of identifying the strength of the speaker's commitment to the truth of the proposition expressed. More generally, it is a matter of establishing how the utterance should be processed. Once again, if the hearer does recover a description of the speaker's intentions it is because she has already understood the utterance. In other words, while the higher-level description that the speaker is making a guess *may* be communicated, it doesn't have to be in order for the hearer to understand the utterance. Sperber and Wilson call acts like guessing (and warning) *non-communicated acts*.

Exercise 1

1 Discuss the difference between promises and threats in terms of the distinction between communicated and non-communicated acts.
2 Explain what is involved in understanding an utterance as prediction.
3 Consider a situation in which I, after strenuously denying your accusation that I have eaten your chocolates, eventually give up and produce the utterance:

OK, it was me.

Is the proposition expressed by this utterance relevant? If not, how else might the utterance be intended to achieve relevance?

6.2 Performatives

Within a traditional speech-act theory framework *explicit performative* utterances like those in (17) are considered to have a special significance for a theory of meaning.

(17) (a) I predict that Jane will leave the room.
(b) I warn you that Jane will leave the room.
(c) I conclude that nouns are verbs.
(d) I promise that I will not smoke.
(e) I bet that Jane will leave the room.

According to Austin (1962: 61, 70), this significance lies in the fact that in each case the performative verb lacks descriptive meaning, or in other words, that it does not contribute to a proposition with truth conditions. Its function is simply to indicate the type of speech act being performed. Austin proposes that performative verbs are only one of a range of devices with this function. For example, he suggests that *probably* in (18a) does the work of *I predict*, while *therefore* in (18b) does the work of *I conclude*.[2]

(18) (a) Probably Jane will leave the room.
(b) Therefore nouns are verbs.

In fact, Austin is unsure whether *conclude* in (17c) is an example of a 'pure performative'. The problem is, as he demonstrates, that it is extremely difficult to provide a workable criterion for distinguishing performative utterances from non-performative (or, as he calls them, *constative*) utterances. Indeed, he eventually abandoned the distinction, so that all utterances are treated as the performances of an act. However, there does seem to be a distinction here – not the one that Austin had in mind, but one which, as we shall see, leads to the rejection of the traditional speech-act view of performatives as non-truth-conditional indicators of speech-act type. [3]

As we shall see in section 6.3, a speaker who presents a proposition as a true description of the world does not necessarily present it as as a proposition whose truth he himself is committed to. Nor does he necessarily expect the hearer to adopt it as one of her own beliefs. Consider, for example, ironic utterances like (19) and examples of reported speech like (20):

(19)   (*Nigel has just insulted Barbara*)
       BARBARA: Nigel is always so nice to me.
(20)   A: What did Jane say?
       B: The prime minister is never going to stand down.

However, let us leave these examples for now, and concentrate on those in which a speaker not only presents a proposition as true, but also indicates that he is committed to its truth.

As we saw in chapter 1, a speaker may be more or less committed to the truth of a proposition, and may or may not indicate the degree of his commitment by linguistic means (consider, for example, the adverb *probably* in (18a)). We shall be returning to this point shortly. The main point here is that in indicating that he is committed to the truth of a proposition a speaker creates expectations of truthfulness, expectations whose strength depends on the degree of commitment the speaker is taken to be conveying, and a hearer may invoke this guarantee as evidence for the truth of the proposition. Exchanges like the one in (21) should be familiar.

(21)   A: How do you know that Jane can knit?
       B: Simon told me.

Of course, just how good this evidence is depends on how much the hearer trusts the speaker (Simon in this case). A more direct and hence less controvertible method of providing evidence would be to produce Jane and get her to do some knitting for A.

Performatives can also be regarded as giving direct (rather than indirect) evidence for the truth of the proposition they express. Thus for example, the speaker of (17a) can be regarded as giving direct evidence for the truth of (22a), the speaker of (17b) can be regarded as giving direct evidence for the truth of (22b), and the speaker of (17c) can be regarded as giving direct evidence for the truth of (22c).

(17) (a) I predict that Jane will leave the room.
      (b) I warn you that Jane will leave the room.
      (c) I conclude that nouns are verbs.
(22) (a) The speaker of (17a) is predicting that Jane will leave the room.
      (b) The speaker of (17b) is warning the hearer that Jane will leave the room.
      (c) The speaker of (17c) is concluding that nouns are verbs.

That is, the speaker of a performative utterance is not so much indicating to the hearer that he believes the proposition it expresses as *showing* the hearer that it is true (in much the same way that Jane can demonstrate that she can knit by knitting).

But this means that performatives do in fact express propositions with truth conditions.[4] On the other hand, it seems that performatives do not generally contribute to the truth conditions of the utterances that contain them. For example, while the speaker of the performative in (17a) (repeated below) can be taken to be communicating the proposition in (22a), it seems that the truth of her utterance hinges on whether or not Jane will leave the room rather than on whether or not the speaker is making a prediction. In other words, although the utterance explicates the higher-level description in (22a), the proposition expressed by her utterance is the one in (23).

(17a) I predict that Jane will leave the room.
(22a) The speaker is predicting that Jane will leave the room.
(23)   Jane will leave the room.

Moreover, it seems that in general a hearer will derive more contextual effects from (23) than she will from (22a), or, in other words, that the main relevance of the utterance in (17a) lies in the embedded proposition. But if this is right, then what *is* the point of saying that you are making a prediction. What is the point of the higher-level proposition?[5]

This question does not arise in the case of utterances like (17d) and (17e) (repeated below) because, as we have seen, the main point of an utterance intended as a bet or a promise does lie in the fact that the speaker is making a bet or a promise.

(17) (d) I promise that I will not smoke.
      (e) I bet that Jane will leave the room.

However, it does arise in the case of (17a) and (17c). And, as Urmson (1966) shows, it can also arise in the case of the so-called psychological verbs like *think* and *know*. Just as the main relevance of (17b) cannot be said to lie in the speaker's description of himself as warning, the main point of (24) cannot be said to lie in the speaker's description of himself as thinking.

(24)   I think that you are wrong.

Urmson calls such verbs *parenthetical verbs* because they can typically occupy parenthetical positions.

(25)   (a)   You are wrong, I think.
       (b)   Jane will, I predict, leave the room.

The fact that they can occupy such positions is not surprising if our analysis is correct and the main relevance of performative utterances and the utterances like (24) lies in their embedded propositions. At the same time, it is not surprising that performative verbs like *bet* typically don't occupy such parenthetical positions. The following utterance is unacceptable:

(26)   Belle d'Azur will win the race, I bet $100. (from Recanati (1987))

Exercise 2

The following utterances might seem to be counter-examples to the claims I have just made:

(a)   He'll forget to come, I bet. (from Urmson (1966))
(b)   I'll come, I promise.

How might such examples be accommodated into our analysis.
A similar problem seems to arise when we compare the following:

(c)   I admit I ate your chocolates.
(d)   I did, I admit, eat your chocolates.

Why would (d) be inappropriate in the situation described above for Exercise 1.3. Notice too the utterance in (e).

(e)   I did, admittedly, eat your chocolates.

Let us return to our original question: what is the point of saying that you are issuing a warning or making a prediction? A clue to the answer lies in two apparently unrelated phenomena. Consider first the text fragments in (27) and (28):

(27)   Do you remember the man who bought your car? Well, he is doing a first year philosophy course.

(28)   Do you see that building over there? Apparently, it's sinking about a foot a year.

The questions in (27) and (28) are not really designed to elicit information. The point of each utterance is to ensure that certain information is available for the interpretation of subsequent utterances. In (27) the speaker is reminding the hearer of information that she already has so that it can be used as context for the interpretation of the next utterance. And in (28) the speaker is simply making sure that the building is salient so that she can refer to it in subsequent utterances.

In these examples the relevance of the first utterance contributes to the relevance by helping the hearer with the processing of the next utterance. That is, we have two acts of communication, one of which is designed primarily to help the hearer with the processing of another. These two acts take place at different times. However, two distinct acts of communication may take place simultaneously. Consider, for example, a situation in which I am giving a cooking demonstration and as I add the milk I produce the utterance in (29):

(29)   I now add the milk.

One act of communication is non-linguistic (that is, the adding of the milk). The point of the linguistic act of communication is to provide a commentary on this non-linguistic act, and thereby constrain the way the audience interprets it.

Sperber and Wilson (1985) have proposed that this is what is going on in the case of many so-called performative utterances. For example, the speaker of (17a) is engaged in two distinct acts of communication. On the one hand, he is communicating the information that Jane will leave the room while on the other he is communicating the information that he is making a prediction. However, the contribution of the second act lies in the way it helps the hearer understand the first act. More specifically, it leads the hearer to understand that the proposition that the speaker is presenting is one about the future and hence one for which he has less than conclusive evidence.

As Urmson (1966) has shown, different parenthetical verbs focus on different aspects of processing. In (17a) the speaker is communicating information about his attitude towards the embedded proposition. In (17b), however, the relevance of the proposition that the speaker is issuing a warning lies in the way it helps the hearer draw the right kind of inferences from the embedded proposition (ones that have to do with the unpleasant or dangerous consequences of the state of affairs it describes). In (17c) the relevance of the higher-level proposition lies in the fact that it helps the hearer see that the embedded proposition is relevant as a proposition which follows logically from some other proposition that has been presented. That is, in these cases the performative verb is focusing on an aspect of utterance interpretation that we shall be examining in Part III.

6.3   Saying, Telling and Asking

So far in this chapter we have been assuming that an utterance which has declarative form expresses a proposition which is relevant as a description of an actual state of affairs. Thus for example, the utterance in (1) (repeated below) will be understood as intended to be relevant as a description of the state of affairs in which there is a snake in the grass.

(1)   There's a snake in the grass.

However, not all declarative utterances are relevant in this way. Consider the utterance in (30):

(30)   You are leaving.

The speaker of (30) could be presenting a proposition which is a description of an actual state of affairs (one in which the hearer is leaving). That is, he could be simply *saying* that the hearer is leaving. However, he might be *telling* the hearer to go. Or he might be *asking* whether the hearer is going. Of course, the speaker may indicate just how he expects the hearer to understand his utterance by using some intonational clue (for example, rising intonation to indicate that he is asking the hearer whether she is going). However, unless the hearer does establish whether the speaker is saying that something is the case, or telling someone to make something the case, or asking whether something is the case, she won't be able to see how the utterance is intended to be relevant at all.

This might seem to suggest that there is a respect in which the speech-act-theory view was right after all. The speaker will not succeed in communicating with the hearer unless he communicates the fact that he is, for example, saying that something is the case. In other words, communication will succeed only if the hearer recovers a description like the one in (31):

(31)   The speaker is saying that the hearer is going.

But are saying that, telling to and asking really speech acts in the sense outlined in traditional speech-act-theory accounts? We might say that *saying* is the most general form of an assertive act, while *telling to* is the most general form of a request for action (a directive), and *asking whether* is the most general form of a request for information. However, defined in this way, these notions cannot play any role in the account of non-declarative utterances. For they do not allow us to maintain any sort of correlation between sentence type and utterance type.

   Searle (1979) defines assertive speech acts as those in which the speaker is committed in some degree to the truth of the proposition his utterance expresses. But in the next section we shall be examining examples of declarative utterances in which the speaker is not committed to the proposition his utterance expresses at all. Recall the examples of irony (19) and reported speech (20):

(19)   (*Nigel has just insulted Barbara*)
       BARBARA: Nigel is always so nice to me.
(20)   A: What did Jane say?
       B: The prime minister is never going to stand down.

In (19) Barbara is presenting the proposition that Nigel is always so nice to her as a description of the world. But she is evidently not committed to its truth. Similarly, although B in (20) is presenting the proposition that the prime minister is never going to stand down as a description of the world, he will not be understood to be reporting one of his own beliefs. If we wish to maintain a correlation between speech-act type and sentence type, we will have to adopt a very weak notion of *saying* which does not involve a commitment to the truth of the proposition expressed. For example, in (19) the speaker is *saying* but not asserting that Nigel is always nice to her.

   As we shall see in sections 6.5 and 6.6, the same kind of points can be made about *telling to* and *asking whether*. However, let me continue to use the example of *saying that* to summarize the arguments of this and the previous sections. A hearer could not understand an utterance at all unless she is able to establish whether it is a case of *saying that, telling to* or *asking whether*. That is, she must integrate the propositional content of the utterance into a higher-level explicature like (31) (repeated here).

(31)   The speaker is saying that the hearer is going.

As we have seen, it will be evident from the context and/or from the linguistic form of the utterance just how strongly committed the speaker is to the truth of the proposition the utterance expresses, and hence how strong a guarantee he is offering for its truth. Clearly, identifying the strength of this guarantee is part of the interpretation process. However, as we have seen in section 6.2, this does not mean that the hearer has to recover a so-called speech-act description (other than *saying telling* and *asking*) in order to understand the utterance. If she does recover such a description it is because she has established the strength of the guarantee the speaker is giving, or, more generally, because she has already established the relevance of the utterance.

  This is not to say that the traditional speech-act type descriptions play no part at all in the comprehension process. Recall promises, bets and confessions (or admissions). However, as we have seen in our discussion of (17d) and (17e) examples, this is not to say that a theory of utterance understanding must include the social and institutional machinery of speech-act theory. In sections 6.5 and 6.6 we shall see that this point applies not just to the interpretation of utterances which have declarative form, but also to the analysis of those utterances which have non-declarative form (for example, imperatives and interrogatives). However, let us stay with declarative form for just a little longer and consider in more detail the cases of saying which cannot be analysed in terms of assertion.

6.4   Interpretive Use

That the utterance in (30) (repeated below) has *declarative form* is a fact about its linguistic properties, and not about its non-linguistic properties. That is, we can say whether a sentence is declarative or not independently of the context in which it is uttered:

(30)   You are leaving.

However, the question of whether this declarative sentence is being used to make an assertion cannot be settled independently of the context. As we have seen, the sentence in (30) could be used to issue an order or to ask a question.

  Within a speech-act framework this means that we can only talk of the speech-act (or illocutionary force) potential of sentences, and that the task of a theory of utterance understanding (pragmatics) is to explain how speakers use contextual information to choose an actual illocutionary force from the potential illocutionary forces associated with the sentence uttered. Thus although it is true that a sentence like (30) may be used to perform something other than an assertion, we can still say that there is a relationship between declarative form and assertive force or that sentences with declarative form are standardly used to perform utterances with assertive force.

As we have seen, Searle (1979) defines an assertive utterance as one which commits the speaker to the truth of the proposition it expresses. As we have seen, commitment to truth comes in varying degrees. Hence the difference between guesses and claims, for example. However, what do we say about the relationship between declarative form and assertive force in view of metaphorical utterances like (32), ironic utterances like (19) and cases of reported speech like (20)?

(32) This room is a pigsty.
(19) (*Nigel has just insulted Barbara*)
      BARBARA: Nigel is always so nice to me.
(20) A: What did Jane say?
      B: The prime minister is never going to stand down.

In none of these cases can we say that the speaker is committed to the truth of the proposition expressed.

According to Recanati (1987), such examples do not prove that there is no relationship between declarative form and assertive force. Rather they demonstrate the need for a *principle of literalness* – that is, a principle which requires speakers to utter a sentence with a certain illocutionary-force potential only if they are trying to perform an act which comes under that potential. Given the contextual assumption that speakers do not want to be misinterpreted, the speaker of, for example, (32) will be understood not to be observing the principle of literalness, and hence cannot be taken to be performing an assertive speech act. Assertive force is indicated, but it is not the *actual* illocutionary force.[6]

Within the framework of speech-act theory, acceptance of the principle of literalness implies that utterances which have declarative form may be interpreted as either genuine assertions or deviant assertions. But the classification of the utterances above as deviant assertions hardly begins to explain what they are taken to convey or how what they convey is recovered. It is true that the speaker of (32), for example, could not be taken to be committed to the literal truth of the proposition his utterance expresses. However, as Sperber and Wilson (1986) argue, this is not to say that such utterances are interpreted by different principles from strictly literal ones. Hearers are not faced with the question of whether an utterance counts as a genuine illocutionary act or not.

Their aim is to recover an interpretation that is consistent with the principle of relevance, and thus the optimally relevant interpretation is not necessarily one in which the proposition expressed is a literal representation of the speaker's opinions or thoughts. Let us examine Sperber and Wilson's arguments in more detail.

The problem in (20) is that the proposition expressed is not a representation of the speaker's own opinion or thought. The speaker is reporting what Jane said, and the utterance will be understood as a representation of what Jane said. Notice that this does not necessarily mean that Jane actually spoke those words. She *might* have produced the utterance in (33). But equally, she might have produced the utterance in (34) or, indeed, the one in (35).

(33)   The prime minister will never stand down.
(34)   She will never stand down.
(35)   Mrs Thatcher? She'll never resign.

B's utterance in (20) is a representation of Jane's utterance (whether that be the one in (33), (34) or (35)) in virtue of the fact that it *resembles* it. In the case where Jane had produced the utterance in (33) the resemblance is very close: B's utterance has the same linguistic form as Jane's. In the case where Jane had produced the utterance in (34) or (35) the resemblance is less faithful. However, in each case there is a resemblance in *content* in the sense that in each case B's utterance shares logical and contextual implications with Jane's. It is not difficult, for example, to think of a context in which *all* these utterances give rise to the same contextual implications. Sperber and Wilson would say that in all three cases B's utterance is relevant as an *interpretation* of Jane's utterance.

This notion of representation by resemblance clearly departs from the more standard truth-conditional notion of descriptive representation in which a proposition is used as a representation of the state of affairs which makes it true. The idea that pictorial representations resemble what they represent is familiar enough. But in fact, all sorts of phenomena can be used representationally. For example, if you want to know how big a kiwi fruit is, I may outline its shape with my fingers or show you another object which I believe has similar proportions. Similarly, you may communicate your wish for a drink in a noisy bar by imitating the act of raising a glass to your lips. Obviously, no two phenomena are exactly alike, and a communicator expects his audience to be able to identify the respects in which the resemblance holds. For example, when I draw a map showing you how to get to my house I do not expect you to walk across a sheet of white paper past signs saying 'pub' and 'supermarket'.

A speaker who intends his utterance to be understood as an interpretation cannot be creating expectations of truthfulness since his utterance does not purport to be a description of a state of affairs. He can only be taken to be raising expectations of *faithfulness*. As we have seen, the degree of faithfulness attempted varies from situation to situation. A fully identical representation is not always the most relevant one. Sometimes a speaker may indicate explicitly what level of faithfulness is being attempted. Compare, for example, (36a) and (36b):

(36) (a) He's bringing a cheesecake. That's precisely what he said.
    (b) He's bringing a cheesecake. At least that's what he gave me to understand.

On other occasions it is left to the hearer to decide just how faithful an interpretation is being offered on the basis of the context and pragmatic principles.

In (36) the speaker is indicating explicitly that the information he is giving is derived from what someone has said. That is, he is indicating the type of evidence that he has for the information he is presenting. Other expressions with a similar function include the underlined expressions in (37):

(37) (a) *Apparently* Nigel is in town.
    (b) *Evidently* Nigel is in town.
    (c) *I gather that* Nigel is in town.
    (d) *They say that* Nigel is in town.

These are lexical devices. However, as a number of writers have reported, there is a wide variety of languages in which speakers use a *hearsay particle* whenever the information they are reporting is obtained from someone else.[7]

Palmer (1986: 51–7, 66–74) analyses such particles as having an essentially modal function. That is, he sees their function in terms of the intention of the speaker to indicate his degree of commitment to the truth of the proposition expressed. Thus the use of the Tuyuca hearsay particle in (38b) indicates that the speaker has less evidence for the truth of the proposition expressed than he does for the truth of the proposition expressed in (38a) where he uses a visual evidential particle:

(38) (a) diiga ape-wi.
        He   played soccer (I saw him).
    (b) diiga ape-yigi.
        He   played soccer (I obtained the information from someone else).
        (Barnes 1984[8])

However, in her study of the role of *ré* and its phonological variant *ri* Blass
(1990: 93–123) argues that this modal analysis leaves many uses of the
hearsay particle *ré* unexplained. For it can be used not only for reporting the
speech of other speakers, but also in attributing thoughts and beliefs. As she
shows in the example given here as (39), the relevance of the utterance does not
always lie simply in the speaker attributing the thought expressed to someone
else. More often it lies in the speaker's attitude to the fact that the speaker has
expressed that thought. Notice in this example that B's utterance does not echo
what A actually says, but rather what he implies:

(39)   A: They [the ants] gather them [grains] and take them out and leave
            them there. They enter the house again, break [the grains] again
            and take them out.
       B: Eh, ants work hard *ré*. (from Blass (1988))

Here the speaker is endorsing what A has said. However, Blass also shows that
a speaker may use *ré* in echoing an utterance in order to dissociate himself from
the opinion echoed.

   This phenomenon is not restricted to Sissala. A similar phenomenon is noted
by Itani-Kaufman in her paper on the Japanese particle *tte* (Itani-Kaufman
1989). As with the Sissala expression *ré*, *tte* is used either as a complementiser
or as a sentence-final particle. In (40) one could say that the function of *tte* is to
indicate that the utterance is to be interpreted as reported speech.

(40)   Kono natsu   atsuka naru   tte.
       this summer hot   become *part*
       I hear that it will be hot this summer.

However, this analysis does not extend to the sort of example in (41) where the
speaker is not only presenting an opinion which is not his own, but also
expressing his disgust towards it:

(41)   Itsumo onaji ne. Donna yogore mo ochiru tte.
       They always say the same thing. Any stain will be removed.

Similarly, Slobin and Aksu (1982) mention that the Turkish morpheme −*mis*,
which is analysed as a hearsay marker, can also be used ironically to cast doubt
upon a proposition.

   Both Blass and Itani-Kaufman have proposed that a more unified account of
hearsay particles can be given in terms of Sperber and Wilson's notion of
representation by resemblance, or interpretive use. Insomuch as they have

reportative function (as in (40)) hearsay particles can be regarded as explicit linguistic indicators of interpretive use. However, an utterance intended as an interpretation does not have to be a representation of what someone has said. It could be an interpretation of someone's thoughts or opinions. For example, free indirect speech, illustrated in the second segment of (42), is interpretive in this sense.

(42)   She walked slowly along the path kicking the papery gold and brown leaves. Yes, autumn was certainly the best season of the year.

Blass reports that the Sissala marker *ré* is used in these sorts of cases. Unfortunately, this use of hearsay particles is not discussed by other authors, and consequently one cannot say just how widespread the phenomenon is. However, as we have seen, a number of linguists have reported the use of hearsay particles in the indication of irony. Let us return to the example in (19) and see how the notion of interpretive use might help us here.

(19)   (*Nigel has just insulted Barbara*)
       BARBARA: Nigel is always so nice to me.

As Sperber and Wilson (1985) have shown, an utterance which is intended as an interpretation is not simply relevant in virtue of the fact that it informs that someone said or thought something. This is illustrated by Blass's example in (39). In reporting someone's thoughts a speaker may indicate her own attitude towards them. Sperber and Wilson call an utterance that is relevant in this way *echoic*. As they show, there is a whole range of attitudes that an echoic utterance may convey. In the following cases (given by Sperber and Wilson) we see an example in which the speaker is endorsing the first speaker's opinion, and then an example in which she is dissociating herself from the opinion echoed.

(43)   HE: It's a lovely day for a picnic.
             (*They go for a picnic and the sun shines*)
       SHE: (*happily*): It's a lovely day for a picnic indeed.
(44)   HE: It's a lovely day for a picnic.
             (*They go for a picnic and it rains*)
       SHE: It's a lovely day for a picnic indeed.

Irony is usually studied as a literary device. And there is nothing literary about the second speaker's utterance in (44). But it is, surely, ironic. We need to say a great deal more about the effects of such utterances, but will leave this until later (see chapter 9). The point here is that irony can be analysed in terms of the interpretive use of representations, and it is not surprising, given this analysis, that hearsay markers can be used to indicate irony.

Notice that according to this analysis, there is nothing deviant about ironic utterances like the one in (19). Certainly, the speaker may be said to have deviated from the truth (or from a standard of literalness). But that is not the point. The speaker's aim is not always to present a true description of a state of affairs. Sometimes his aim is to express his attitude towards an opinion that a particular person or people in general hold. And the optimally relevant means of doing this will often be to echo that opinion and indicate (perhaps by non-linguistic means like the tone of his voice, the look on his face) that he is dissociating himself from it.

Exercise 3

Irony is standardly analysed in terms of meaning the opposite of what one says. How well does this analysis account for the following examples?

(a)   Being an invalid, Joseph Sedley contented himself with a bottle of claret besides his Madeira before dinner, and he managed a couple of plates full of strawberries and cream, and twenty four little rout cakes that were lying neglected in a plate near him. (Thackeray, *Vanity Fair*)

(b)   The Penguins had the finest army in the world and so did the Porpoises. (Anatole France, *Penguin Island*)

(c)   Oh to be in England
      Now that April's there.

                                   (said on a cold, wet spring day)

Finally, in this section let us return to the example in (32).

(32)   This room is a pigsty.

Readers will recognize this as an example of metaphor – not, of course, the sort of metaphor which you find in poetry or drama, but a metaphor none the less. We shall be discussing the question of what makes a metaphor more or less poetic in chapter 9. Our task here is to show why such utterances should not be analysed as deviant assertions as, for example, Recanati (1987) argues, but rather as utterances which are consistent with the principle of relevance.

Clearly, (32) would have to be regarded as deviant if literalness were a standard in communication. However, the following sorts of examples (based on ones given by Sperber and Wilson (1986)) suggest that this is not the case.

(45)   You have met a friend you haven't seen for years and during the conversation she asks you (perhaps rather impertinently) how much you earn. In fact, you earn £897.56 a month. However, your answer is:
£900 a month.

(46)   You are filling in your tax return and you are required to state your monthly salary. This time your answer is:
£897.56.

I trust that these would be the answers you would give in the circumstances described, and you agree that you would get away with the strictly false answer in (45), but not in (46). Moreover, I trust that you agree that the strictly true answer would be inappropriate in (48). How do we account for this?

What difference would it have made had you answered £897.56 in (45)? The hearer would have obtained the same effects (for example, you probably can afford a mortgage, or holidays in Europe, a car). However, the cost of obtaining those effects would have been greater than the cost incurred through processing the answer £900. In other words, you answered as you did in (45) because this was the optimally relevant answer – the one consistent with the principle of relevance. Literalness is only one way of optimizing relevance.

Sperber and Wilson call this sort of phenomenon *loose talk*, and suggest that metaphorical uses of language can be understood in essentially the same way. A speaker presents an utterance as an interpretation of a thought. This may be an interpretation of someone else's thought, as for example in the case of free indirect speech, hearsay or irony. Or it may be an interpretation of the speaker's own thought. Here of course the hearer may be guided by the linguistic form of the utterance (see above), or she may have to work out the speaker's intentions on the basis of the context and the principle of relevance. In neither case does the proposition expressed have to be *identical* to the thought that it represents. The optimally relevant representation of the thought might be one which does not fully reproduce it.

Let us apply this analysis to the utterance in (32). The utterance is intended as an interpretation of the speaker's own thought. However, it is very unlikely that the hearer will regard the proposition it expresses as a literal interpretation of that thought. That is, she will take the speaker to be committed to a thought which resembles the proposition expressed or, in other words, a thought which is represented by the proposition expressed.

This analysis raises a number of questions. For example, we have not discussed the question of the effects that figurative utterances convey. We have established that the speaker is not committed to the truth of the proposition expressed by such an utterance, or, in other words, that the proposition expressed by a figurative utterance cannot be regarded as an explicature. And we have established that this does not mean that figurative utterances are deviant assertions, but that they are relevant as interpretive representations. But we have not addressed the question of the effects that a speaker expects to gain by presenting a thought in this way. As we shall see, the answers to all these questions have more to do with implicature than with explicature, and accordingly, we shall have to postpone this discussion until chapter 9.

6.5   Non-Declarative Utterances: Imperatives

Within the framework of speech-act theory the use of the imperative mood, illustrated in (47), is associated with the performance of speech acts of the *directive* type – for example, ordering, requesting, entreating, insisting and advising.

(47)   Leave the room.

These acts are defined as attempts to get the hearer to do something, and the differences between them are regarded as differences of strength. Thus for example, an order is a stronger type of directive than a request. As we have seen, in this framework a hearer does not understand an utterance unless she can identify the type of speech act the speaker intended to perform. This means that after identifying (47) as a directive the hearer must then recover a description such as (48).

(48)   The speaker is requesting the hearer to leave the room.

In this section we shall see that understanding an utterance like (47) does not necessarily involve the recovery of a speech-act description like (48). It is true that in order to establish the relevance of an utterance a hearer has to be able to decide whether the speaker was expressing the belief that a certain proposition was true, whether he was echoing some other person's belief (see section 6.4) or whether he was expressing the desirability of a proposition being true. That is, she has to decide whether the utterance is an example of *saying that* or an example of *telling to*. However, this does not mean that the hearer has to recover a *speech-act* description. In particular, it does not mean that the speaker of an utterance intended as an example of *telling to* was intending to get the hearer to do something. The examples that follow are, of course, analogous to the ones in (19), (20) and (32).

(49) That's right. Misinterpret everything I say.
(50) A: What did Jane say?
      B: Vote National.
(51) Reach for the stars.

In none of these cases could the speaker be regarded as expressing *his* attitude of desire. In (49) he is dissociating himself from the view that the state of affairs represented by the proposition expressed by his utterance is desirable probably with the intention of ridiculing this attitude. In (50) he is reporting what someone else (Jane) told him to do. And in (51) he cannot be construed as literally telling the hearer to reach for the stars. All these cases can be explained in terms of the notion of interpretive use outlined in section 6.4. Although the utterance can be identified as a case of telling to, the speaker will not be understood to be attempting to get the hearer to do something.

For the remainder of this section we shall restrict the discussion to examples of telling to in which the speaker is expressing his own attitude of desire and where the proposition expressed is a literal representation of the state of affairs viewed as desirable. That is, we shall be restricting the discussion to literal utterances. However, as Wilson and Sperber (1988) point out, there are many examples of imperative utterances which cannot be regarded as non-literal or non-serious, but which also cannot be regarded as attempts to get the hearer to do something. All the following examples are taken or adapted from Schmerling (1982) and Wilson and Sperber (1988).

(52) *Advice*
      Recipe for cheese sauce: Melt two ounces of butter in a saucepan. Add four tablespoons of flour, and then gradually pour in eight fluid ounces of previously warmed milk, stirring continuously . . .

There is no sense in which the writer of this recipe could be regarded as attempting to get the reader to perform these actions since she does not know or care whether the reader will perform them.

(53) *Permission*
      A: Can I open the window? I'm really hot.
      B: Go on, open it then.

Again there is no reason to think that the speaker cares whether the hearer brings about the state of affairs described, and hence no reason to analyse his utterance in terms of an attempt to get the hearer to do something.

(54)   *Threats and dares*
       Mary, on seeing Peter about to throw a snowball, says threateningly:
       Go on. Just you dare.

Here Mary's utterance is an attempt to get Peter *not* to do something.

(55)   *Good wishes*
       Get well soon.

Getting well soon is not under the hearer's control, and consequently, it would be odd to regard this utterance as an attempt to get the hearer to get well.

(56)   *Audienceless cases*
       Please don't rain.

This example needs no explanation.

(57)   *Predetermined cases*
       A child is sent to apologize to someone and says to himself as he approaches the door:
       Please be out.

As in (56), there is no hearer. Furthermore the event described has already happened (or not happened).

The idea that a proposition may be true either in the actual world or in other possible worlds is familiar from formal semantics (for example, Lewis (1972)). [9] In Sperber and Wilson's framework this distinction is presented in psychological terms. A proposition may be entertained as a description of the actual world or as a description of another possible world. However, in addition, they introduce two new notions which, they claim, play a role in the analysis of imperatives. First, they claim that a proposition may be entertained as a state of affairs in a *potential* world – that is, a world that is compatible with the individual's assumptions about the actual world. Second, they claim that a proposition may be entertained as a description of a state of affairs in a desirable world. On the basis of this, they go on to propose that imperative sentences are used to indicate that a state of affairs is both potential and desirable. [10]

That we are restricting ourselves to so-called serious cases means we are only considering those cases in which the speaker regards the state of affairs described as desirable and potential. But as Wilson and Sperber emphasize, desirability is a three-place relation. X regards Y as desirable to Z. A speaker may be indicating that the state of affairs described is desirable to himself. But equally, he may be indicating that it is desirable to the hearer. This means that in interpreting an imperative utterance the hearer has to establish from whose point of view the state of affairs is desirable – the speaker's or the hearer's.

In the case of orders, requests, pleas, good wishes and what Wilson and Sperber call the audienceless and predetermined examples the hearer will understand the utterance as representing a state of affairs that is desirable from the speaker's point of view. The various subcases are distinguished from each other by the different sorts of contextual assumptions that are brought to bear on the interpretation process. For example, if it is evident that the hearer is in a position to bring about the state of affairs described, then the utterance may be understood as a request, order or plea. Orders are distinguished from pleas and requests by contextual assumptions about the social relationship between the speaker and hearer. Thus if the speaker is evidently in a position of authority over the hearer, the utterance will be understood as an order. The difference between requests and pleas is essentially a difference in the degree to which the state of affairs described is presented as desirable. Thus if the speaker of (47) is understood to be indicating that the hearer's leaving the room is extremely desirable from his (the speaker's) point of view, then he will be understood to be begging (or pleading) rather than requesting.

Good wishes are distinguished from requests, orders and pleas by the fact that it is evident to the hearer that the speaker believes, first, that neither he nor the hearer is in a position to bring about the state of affairs described, and, second, that this state of affairs would be beneficial to the hearer. The audienceless and predetermined cases are distinguished from good wishes by the fact that, first, there need be no hearer present, and, second, the state of affairs is beneficial to the speaker.

If the hearer understands the speaker to be indicating that the state of affairs is desirable from the hearer's point of view, then the utterance will be understood as permission or advice. If the speaker of (47) is understood simply to be indicating that leaving would be desirable from the hearer's point of view, then the utterance will be understood as advice. If the speaker is understood to be conceding that leaving is desirable to the hearer *and* guaranteeing that this is possible, then the utterance will be understood as permission.

Notice that in none of these cases is it necessary for the hearer to produce a speech-act description of the speaker's intentions. If the hearer does understand (47) as an order rather than advice, it is because the optimally relevant interpretation is one in which the state of affairs described is desirable from the speaker's point of view. And if, for example, she understands it as an order rather than a plea, it is because the optimally relevant interpretation is one in which she must bring to bear certain contextual assumptions regarding the speaker's social position.

6.6   Non-Declarative Utterances: Interrogatives

Within the standard speech-act-theory framework interrogatives like the ones in (60) and (61) are analysed as having the force of questions which are, in turn, analysed as requests for information.[11]

(58)   When are you going to leave?
(59)   Are you going to leave?

In the case of the *yes–no* question in (59) the information requested is essentially the truth value of its propositional content. However, in the case of *wh-questions* the information requested corresponds to the value of a variable, which in the case of (58) is *at some time*.

The problem is that many interrogative utterances cannot be analysed as requests for information. Wilson and Sperber (1988) draw attention to the following sort of examples, many of which are discussed by Bell (1975):

(60)   *Exam questions*
EXAMINER: Who discovered New Zealand?

The examiner is not asking this question because he wants to know the answer, but because he wants to assess the candidate's attempt at an answer.

(61)   *Expository questions*
What are the objections to this analysis? First, . . .

Here the speaker goes on to answer the question himself.

(62)   *Rhetorical questions*
Am I always going to have to pick up your clothes?

The speaker of (62) is not expecting any answer at all.

(63)   *Speculative questions/musings*
       Now, who is going to win the by-election tomorrow?

According to the speech-act account, there is no point in asking a question unless you think that the hearer can provide the answer. But the speaker of (63) may know that he doesn't know the answer, and he may know that the hearer doesn't know the answer. Indeed, he may know that no one knows the answer (at the time of the utterance).

(64)   *Guess questions*
       The speaker holds an object in his hand, places his hands behind his back, and asks:
       Which hand is it in?

Since the speaker already knows the answer, his question cannot be a request for information. Moreover, there is no way in which the hearer can *know* the answer; the answer can only be a guess.

Utterances are relevant in virtue of what they represent. As we have seen in this chapter, there are various ways in which an utterance may represent, and, correspondingly, various ways in which an utterance may be relevant. An ordinary assertion, for example, is relevant as a (descriptive) representation of a state of affairs. An order is relevant as a representation of a desirable state of affairs. And both declarative and imperative utterances may be relevant as an interpretation either of another utterance or of a thought. What, then, does an interrogative utterance represent?

The point of a question is, surely, to indicate that its answer is relevant. In other words, the relevance of a question derives from its indication that its answer would be relevant. I would not ask the question in (59) if I believed the answer was not relevant to me. In other words, in asking the question I am creating expectations about the relevance of its answer. This suggests that a question achieves relevance by representing its answer. That is, it is relevant in virtue of being an interpretation of a relevant thought – namely, its answer.

However, as the rhetorical and expository examples show, a speaker who asks a question does not always regard its answer as relevant to himself. On the contrary, the impression given by these speakers is that they have information to *give*. That is, their questions are relevant as interpretations of answers which they believe to be relevant to the hearer.

The distinction we are drawing here is analogous to the one we drew for imperatives. In the case of an imperative the hearer's task is to make an assumption about the identity of the person to whom the speaker regards the state of affairs represented as being desirable. In the case of an interrogative her task is to identify the individual to whom the speaker regards the thought represented as being desirable (relevant).

In the case of requests for information, exam questions, self-addressed and speculative questions the speaker is indicating that the answer is relevant to himself. As with imperatives, subtypes are distinguished by the different contextual assumptions that the hearer is expected to bring to bear on their interpretation. Thus for example, if it is evident to the hearer that the speaker of (65) has not noticed that she is in the room, then she will understand the utterance as a self-addressed question.

(65)   Where is the whisky?

If it is evident to the hearer that the speaker realizes that he is a better position to answer his question than she is (because he has hidden it), then (65) would be relevant because it is a request for an answer which is relevant not so much for the evidence it provides about the whereabouts of the whisky, but more for what it indicates about the hearer's beliefs about the whereabouts of the whisky, or her ability to predict the speaker's actions.

As we have seen section 6.5, a representation which is used to interpret another representation need not be identical to it. Thus, for example, an utterance which is used as an interpretation of the speaker's thought may resemble that thought only in certain respects – recall metaphorical utterances here. In the case of a yes–no question the proposition expressed is in fact identical to the proposition expressed by the answer. Thus the question in (59) (repeated below) expresses the proposition in (66).

(59)   Are you going to leave?

(66)   You are going to leave.

Exercise 4

1   Try to give an explanation for exam questions along similar lines.

2   What are the differences between the following questions?

   (a)   Are you going to leave? (= 59)
   (b)   Aren't you going to leave?
   (c)   Are you going to leave or not?

Do they all express the same proposition?
Would they all be relevant in the same sort of context?
Illustrate your answer here with examples.

Note: According to Katz and Postal (1964), yes–no questions are truncated versions of alternative questions like (c). This means that (a), (b) and (c) would be semantically equivalent. Also see Bolinger (1978).

In contrast with yes–no questions, wh-questions do not express full proposi- tions. In each of the following the wh-phrase can be thought of as a variable which has to be filled in order to obtain a complete proposition with a truth value. That is, in each of the following the question in (a) represents the completion of the incomplete propositional form in (b):

(67) (a) When are you going to leave? (= 58)
      (b) You are leaving *when*
(68) (a) Where are you going?
      (b) You are going *where*
(69) (a) Who are you going with?
      (b) You are going with *who(m)*

But, of course, to provide a value for the variable is to give an answer to the question. In other words, the speaker of a wh-question expresses an in- complete proposition and indicates that its completion would be a relevant answer.

   In this chapter we have seen that there is a link between sentence type and pragmatic interpretation. Declarative sentences are linked with *saying that,* imperative sentences are linked with *telling to,* and interrogative sentences with *asking whether.* But this is not a link between sentence types and speech-act types, as they are defined in the traditional speech-act framework. *Saying that, telling to* and *asking whether* are not institutional or social acts in the way that bidding at bridge, betting and promising are, and that they play an essential role in communication does not demonstrate how language is embedded in social institutions. Rather, they are analysed in psychological terms. *Saying that* is analysed in terms of the communication of a thought which is entertained as a description of an actual state of affairs; *telling to* is analysed in terms of the communication of a thought which is is entertained as a description of a state of affairs that is potential and desirable; and *asking whether* is analysed in terms of the communication of a proposition which is entertained as an interpretation of a desirable thought.

   As we have seen, a declarative sentence is not necessarily used to communi- cate a thought which is entertained by the speaker. Nor is it necessarily used to express a proposition which is identical with the thought entertained by the speaker. Recall the examples of irony in (19) and metaphor in (32):

(19)   (*Nigel has just insulted Barbara*)
        BARBARA: Nigel is always so nice to me.

(32)   This room is a pigsty.

Similar remarks apply to imperatives and interrogatives. Consider the example of irony in (49), the example of free indirect speech in (70) and the examples of metaphor in (51) and (71).

(49)   That's right. Misinterpret everything I say.
(51)   Reach for the stars.
(70)   She closed her eyes. Would he ever stop talking?
(71)   Would their friendship blossom?

According to the account given in this chapter, these are not deviations from a norm of literalness, but simply exemplify different ways in which an utterance may achieve relevance. However, whether an utterance is or is not echoic, and the degree to which the proposition it expresses, are not matters that can be determined by its linguistically encoded semantic representation. These matters must be decided on the basis of contextual clues and the principle of relevance. In other words, linguistic indicators like declarative, imperative and interrogative mood serve only to indicate the *direction* in which the relevance of the utterance lies.[12]

Recommended Reading

Speech Acts and Relevance Theory

Sperber and Wilson 1986: ch. 4, 243–55.
Wilson and Sperber 1988.

The Traditional Speech-Act Framework

Austin 1962.
Searle 1969: especially chs 1–3.
Searle 1979 (classification of speech acts).
Bach and Harnish 1979: ch. 3 (classification of speech acts).

Performatives

Austin 1962: especially pp. 53–82 (traditional speech-act aproach).
Searle 1989 (a revised speech-act approach).
Recanati 1987: especially pp. 117–207 (a revised speech-act approach)
Blakemore 1991 (a relevance-theoretic approach).

Non-Declarative Sentences: Imperatives

Bell 1975.
Huntley 1984.
B. Clark 1989 (pseudo-imperatives).

Non-Declarative Sentences: Interrogatives

Schmerling 1982.
Bolinger 1978.

Evidentials

Palmer 1986: 66–75 (general discussion).
Blass 1990: 93–123 (a relevance-theoretic approach).

Notes

1 See also Searle (1979).
2 For a more detailed examination of this distinction and Austin's analysis of performatives, see Recanati (1987: 15, 20–5, 31–43, 67–86).
3 The following argument is given by Sperber and Wilson (1985). Recanati (1987) also believes that Austin was wrong to abandon the distinction between constatives and performatives, and, moreover, that performatives should not be analysed as non-truth-conditional indicators of illocutionary force (speech-act type). However, his analysis of performatives is still a speech-act theoretic one in that it assumes that a speaker must communicate the type of speech act he is performing. Recanati's distinction between performatives and constatives owes a great deal to Searle (1979) who makes a distinction between those utterances with word-to-world direction of fit and those with double direction of fit. That is, whereas in constative utterances the speaker's aim is to describe the state of affairs it represents, in performative utterances his aim is to bring about the state of affairs it represents. Searle (1989) makes the point that while all utterances (including assertions) are *performances*, not all utterances are *performative* according to this criterion.
4 Recanati (1987) and Searle (1989) argue that explicit performatives have truth conditions, but analyse them as declarations which are true in virtue of creating the

states of affairs they represent. In contrast with the analysis being outlined here, both analyses assume that the classification of speech acts plays an essential role in communication, so that what is communicated by an utterance includes its assignment to a particular speech-act type.

5 The discussion which follows has been adapted from Blakemore (1991).

6 Recanati claims that this distinction corresponds to Austin's distinction between locutionary and illocutionary acts. This interpretation of Austin should be contrasted with that of Searle who identifies locutionary meaning with propositional content.

Recanati's appeal to a principle of literalness might be derived from Grice's approach to the interpretation of figurative utterances (originally set out in his 1967 William James Lectures, and later in Grice (1989)) in which figurative utterances are analysed in terms of deliberate flouting of the maxim of truth. As we shall see later in this section, it is not clear that the assumption underlying this analysis – namely, that truth (or literalness) is a standard in communication – can be maintained.

7 See, for example, Derbyshire (1979) for a description of hearsay particles in Hixkaryana, Barnes (1984) for a description of evidentials in Tuyuca, Slobin and Aksu (1982) for an analysis of hearsay particles in Turkish, Donaldson (1980) for a description of hearsay particles in Ngiyamba.

8 In fact, Barnes reports that Tuyuca (a language spoken in Brazil and Colombia) has a system of five evidentials: visual, non-visual, apparent, hearsay and assumed.

9 For an introduction to this distinction, as it is made in formal semantics, see Allwood, Andersson and Dahl (1977: 22–3).

10 This proposal should be contrasted with that made by Huntley (1984), who claims that imperatives should be treated as semantically equivalent to infinitivals. More particularly, imperatives 'represent a situation as being merely envisaged as a possibility with no commitment as to whether it obtains in past, present or future, in *this* world' (p. 122). As Wilson and Sperber (1988) point out, it is difficult to see why a hearer should conclude just from the fact that the speaker is envisaging a state of affairs as a possibility that he is being requested, advised or permitted to bring it about.

11 See, for example, Searle (1979) and Bach and Harnish (1979: 40–8).

12 This account of non-declarative sentences has ignored a range of phenomena, for example, other sentence types (exclamatives, optatives, hortatives), embedded questions, pseudo-imperatives, threats. See Sperber and Wilson (1986: 253) for an outline of how exclamatives may be analysed along the same lines as interrogatives. See B. Clark (1989: 53–74) for an analysis of pseudo-imperatives.

Part III Implicature

7 Types of Implicature

7.1 Introduction

Every communicator is aware – often too painfully aware – that there is more than one way of communicating a message. Writers may agonize over their choice of words. Speakers may regret their choice of words. And both writers and speakers have to decide just how much of what they want to communicate needs to be put into words at all. Clearly, writers have more time for such decisions than speakers. However, it is a decision that any communicator has to make.

In Part II we considered various ways in which the *proposition expressed* by an utterance may be more or less explicit. For example, we saw how the hearer of an utterance like (1) must go beyond its linguistic meaning in order to recover a proposition which will yield adequate contextual effects.

(1) Your paper is too long.

Thus, for example, on the basis of her contextual assumptions the hearer might derive the enriched form in (2):

(2) The article that the hearer has written is too long for the conference.

However, although the hearer uses contextual – that is, non-linguistic – information in order to derive (2), she uses this information to build on the blueprint provided by the grammar. That is, there is a connection between the linguistic properties of the utterance and the proposition she recovers. In contrast, there is no connection between the linguistic properties of B's utterance in (3) and the proposition (represented in (4)) that the hearer will derive as B's answer to A's question.

(3) A: Did I get invited to the conference?
    B: Your paper was too long.
(4) Speaker A did not get invited to the conference.

The hearer derives (4) from the proposition which she takes the speaker to have expressed, which in the context of A's question will be the one in (2), together with contextual assumptions such as the one in (5):

(5) If your paper is too long for the conference you will not be invited.

In other words, (4) can be derived only once the hearer has derived the proposition expressed by the utterance.

As we have seen, Sperber and Wilson call assumptions that are derived in this way *implicatures*. In this chapter we shall be examining various types of implicated information. But first, let us consider a question that is raised by the example in (3): On what grounds is the speaker entitled to expect that the hearer will recover the implicature in (4)? Why, for example, doesn't she recover the assumption in (6) instead?

(6) Nigel will not attend the conference.

Because (6) simply doesn't follow from (2)? But (4) doesn't follow from (2) either. It only follows from (2) taken together with the contextual assumption in (5). It is in principle possible for the hearer to combine (2) with a wide variety of contextual assumptions. It might, for example, be possible for the hearer to access the contextual assumptions in (7).

(7) (a) If your paper is too long for the conference, you will not be invited.
     (b) If you are not invited to the conference, there will be no papers on pragmatics.
     (c) If there are no papers on pragmatics at the conference, Nigel will not attend.

Why would a hearer who was able to access such assumptions still be less likely to derive (6) as an implicature than (4)?

Recall that the principle of relevance entitles the hearer to expect that she can obtain adequate contextual effects for a minimum cost in processing. Processing costs are affected by the cost of accessing and using the context, so that the larger and less accessible the context, the greater the processing cost. In the example under discussion B's utterance provides the hearer with immediate access to a context which yields a contextual effect – that is, the context in (5). It is true that this context could be extended, as in (7) for example, to obtain further contextual effects. However, since the context in (5) did yield adequate contextual effects, the hearer is entitled to assume that this is the interpretation intended by the speaker. As we have seen, having found an interpretation that yields adequate effects for no unjustifiable effort in a way the speaker could have manifestly foreseen, the hearer is entitled to accept this, and only this, as the intended interpretation.

But this seems to raise a further question: Why would a speaker aiming at optimal relevance produce the utterance in (3) as an answer to A's question, rather than the utterance in (8)?

(8)   You are not invited to the conference.

For, surely, in producing the indirect answer, the speaker has required the hearer to access the context in (5) and to deduce (4) as a contextual implication. Each of these steps requires processing effort which would not have been required for the interpretation of the direct answer in (8). How can we reconcile this with the assumption that the speaker was being optimally relevant?

We need to recall here that according to the principle of relevance, an utterance is optimally relevant only if it puts the hearer to no unjustifiable effort in achieving the contextual effects. This suggests that the hearer of B's utterance in (3) can maintain her assumption that it is consistent with the principle of relevance only if she assumes that B intended to achieve more effects than would have been achieved by the direct answer in (8). For example, it is likely that B may believe that A will want to know *why* he has not been invited to the conference. Or perhaps he is trying to make A feel better about not being invited by making sure that he knows that the problem was not that the paper was bad. In fact, it is not necessary that B knows exactly what effects the hearer will recover. He must simply believe that it is worthwhile for the hearer to undertake the extra processing entailed by the indirect answer, because it will lead to increased effects.

7.2   Implicated Premises and Implicated Conclusions

As we have just seen, the decision of the speaker of this utterance to convey his message implicitly and produce an indirect answer to A's question rather than a direct one forced the hearer to access the contextual assumption in (5) and combine it with the proposition expressed to derive the conclusion in (4).

(5)   If your paper is too long for the conference you will not be invited.
(4)   Speaker A did not get invited to the conference.

In other words, both these assumptions must be recovered by the hearer in order to satisfy herself that the utterance is consistent with the principle of relevance. Accordingly, Sperber and Wilson propose that both assumptions – that is, the contextual assumption and the conclusion – should be regarded as implicatures of the utterance. They call (5) an *implicated assumption* (or *implicated premise*) and (4) an *implicated conclusion*.

So the fact that B produced the utterance he did indicates that he expected the hearer to supply the assumption in (5). It is possible, of course, that the hearer would already have (5) among her existing assumptions. Then the effect of B's utterance would be either to strengthen or to confirm her belief in its factuality (or truth).

However, as we have seen, the assumptions that the hearer brings to bear on the interpretation of an utterance are not always retrieved ready-made from memory (or deduced from existing assumptions). In some cases the hearer will construct the context for the interpretation of an utterance as part of its interpretation. In other words, the context is not, as some writers have assumed,[1] given in advance of the comprehension process, but rather constructed as a part of it. Let us consider a different example.

Barbara and I are listening to some music. I do not know what it is or, indeed, anything about it, and she is aware of my ignorance. Nevertheless she may justifiably expect me to interpret her answer in (9) as implicating the conclusion in (10).

(9) ME: Do you like this music?
     BARBARA: I've never liked atonal music.
(10) Barbara does not like this music

The hearer will have to supply the contextual assumption in (11) in order to derive an interpretation that is consistent with the principle of relevance.

(11) The music we are listening to is atonal.

Once again it is logically possible that the hearer could supply any of a wide range of contextual assumptions that are accessible to her and thus derive a wide variety of contextual implications. However, this is not psychologically possible. Given her assumption that the utterance is consistent with the principle of relevance, she will interpret it in the smallest and most accessible context that yields adequate contextual effects. As long as I have a strategy for constructing the assumption in (11) given an exchange of the form in (9), it is of little importance whether I believed that (11) was true in advance of the exchange. And as long as this strategy yields an overall interpretation consistent with the principle of relevance, Barbara is entitled to assume that I will interpret her answer in the context of (11) even though she knows that I did not have this assumption available in advance of her utterance.

What is Barbara trying to achieve by producing this answer rather than the direct one? For if her utterance is consistent with the principle of relevance, she must be trying to achieve something. There are various possibilities: he might be hoping to educate me by indicating what atonal music sounds like; she might be encouraging me to share her opinion that atonal music is unpleasant; she might be trying to impress me by showing that *she* knows what atonal music sounds like; she might be trying to display her extensive musical knowledge and discriminating taste. As in the earlier example, it is not necessary that Barbara has any sharply delimited intention here. All that matters is that the implicated assumption in (11) has some relevance.

We shall be returning to this point below. However, let us here recall the phenomena known as *bridging implicatures* (discussed in chapter 5). These are implicatures needed to establish the reference of a referring expression in a following utterance. Thus the hearer of (12) and (13) will supply the contextual assumptions in (14) and (15) respectively, even if there had been no previous mention of the number of lights in the room.

(12) (a) She went into the room.
     (b) The light was on.
(13) (a) She went into the room.
     (b) Both of the lights were on.

(14) The room had a light.
(15) The room had two lights.

Wilson and Sperber (1986) suggest that the interpretation of these utterances might proceed along the following lines. From her encyclopaedic knowledge of rooms, a hearer will know that it is possible for a room to have one, two or several lights. That is, she will be able to construct the assumptions in (14) and (15), but will not know in advance of the utterance which of them is true. On the assumption that the speaker of, say, (13) is aiming at optimal relevance, she will realize that she must construct the assumption in (15) and use it to establish the reference of *both of the lights* in (13b). If this yields an adequate number of contextual effects for no unjustifiable effort, she will assume that this is the interpretation intended by the speaker and hence that the speaker takes the responsibility for the truth of (15). As we saw in chapter 5, the role of the implicated assumption is not to yield contextual effects, but to enable the hearer to recover the proposition expressed by the utterance, which is, of course, a prerequisite for recovering any contextual effects at all.

7.3   Strong and Weak Implicatures

We began this chapter with the observation that all communicators – speakers and writers – must make a decision about how much of what they want to communicate they are going to communicate explicitly and how much they are going to leave implicit. Since the recovery of implicitly conveyed information depends on the contextual assumptions that are brought to bear, this decision inevitably depends on the speaker's estimation of the hearer's contextual resources. A speaker who is aiming at optimal relevance must assume that the contextual assumptions required for the interpretation of the utterance are immediately accessible to the hearer.

In the examples we have considered so far there is no difficulty about this. For the hearer is given very little choice about the contextual assumptions she should bring to bear on the interpretation process. It is true that she could in principle access a wide variety of contextual assumptions and use them to recover a wide variety of contextual implications. However, as we have seen, this is not a real – that is, psychologically real – possibility. Given her assumption that the utterance is consistent with the principle of relevance, there is at most one context (or type of context) that she could choose and at most one interpretation (or type of interpretation) she could recover.

This suggests that the speaker is exploiting the hearer's assumption that the utterance is consistent with the principle of relevance in order to *constrain* her interpretation. For example, the effect of the indirect answers in (3) and (9) is to constrain the hearer's interpretation by making a contextual assumption immediately accessible, thus ensuring correct context selection at minimal processing cost.

In contrast, the hearer of the direct answer in (16) is free to interpret it in any way she likes.

(16)   A: Did I get invited to the conference?
       B: No, you didn't.

Obviously, that A asked the question gives B grounds for assuming that she has immediate access to some context in which the information he is presenting is relevant. However, the form of B's utterance indicates that he has no particular idea of what exactly this context is. In other words, while B's utterance is optimally relevant, it does not communicate any implicatures at all.

Here we have two extremes: the case of the indirect answer and its implicature in (4), where it is impossible to see how the speaker could have been aiming at optimal relevance unless he expected the hearer to access a specific contextual assumption and to derive a specific conclusion; and the case in (16) where the speaker has no previous expectations at all about the way his utterance will be interpreted. In the first case the utterance will have fully determinate implicatures, while in the second it will have no implicatures at all.

In between these two extremes there is a range of intermediate cases. For example, we have already seen in the case of the indirect answers in (3) and (9) how a speaker can encourage the hearer to supply contextual assumptions of a certain type and thus to derive a certain type of conclusion, but not care which specific assumptions are supplied and which specific conclusion is derived. Thus in (9) Barbara could have offered the indirect answer (repeated here as (17)) in the expectation that I would access an assumption along the lines of the one in (18) and derive a conclusion along the lines of the one in (19).

(17)　I've never liked atonal music.
(18)　People who know what atonal music is are very knowledgeable.
(19)　Barbara is very knowledgeable.

This is not necessarily the interpretation that Barbara specifically intended. It is simply a line of interpretation that is suggested by her utterance. As we saw, there are other possible lines of interpretation. At the same time, the hearer is not completely free in her choice of contextual assumptions (and hence in the derivation of conclusions) as she was in the case of (16). In other words, although the utterance does not have a fully determinate implicature, there is a range of possible implicatures, any of which which would enable the hearer to maintain her assumption that the utterance is consistent with the principle of relevance.

This suggests that implicatures may be more or less determinate, or as Sperber and Wilson put it, more or less strong. The strongest implicatures are those fully determinate implicated conclusions and premises that the hearer is forced to derive in order to obtain an interpetation consistent with the principle of relevance. The tighter the constraint the speaker imposes on the hearer's choice of contextual assumptions, the stronger the resulting implicatures. The less tight the constraint, the weaker the resulting implicatures. And where there is no constraint at all on the hearer's choice of contextual assumptions, the utterance has no implicatures.

That implicatures may be indeterminate was recognized by Grice when he first introduced the notion:

> Since to calculate a conversational implicature is to calculate what has to be supposed in order to preserve the supposition that the Co-operative Principle has been observed, and since there may be various possible specific explanations, a list of which may be open, the conversational

implicatum in such cases will be a disjunction of such specific explanations; and if the list of these is open, the implicatum will have just the kind of indeterminacy that many actual implicata do in fact seem to possess. (1975: 58)

Some writers (for example, Leech 1983: 31–44) have taken this to mean that inferential accounts of utterance interpretation must be abandoned in favour of probabilistic or informal accounts. However, in Sperber and Wilson's account the recovery of *all* implicatures – weak or strong – involves the same inferential processes. The hearer supplies specific contextual assumptions and derives specific contextual effects. In every case the hearer's interpretation is constrained by her assumption that the utterance is consistent with the principle of relevance. What varies is the degree of specificity of the speaker's expectations about the way that optimal relevance will be achieved, and hence, the degree of responsibility that he must take for the particular contextual assumptions made and the particular conclusions derived. For example, since Barbara (in (9)), could not have expected her utterance to be optimally relevant without expecting me to supply the assumption in (11) to derive the contextual implication in (10), she must take as much responsibility for the truth of these assumptions as for the truth of the proposition that her utterance explicitly expressed. That is, she could be justifiably accused of having misled me should it transpire that she did in fact like the music we were listening to. On the other hand, it would not be justifiable for me to accuse her of misleading me should it transpire that she was not in fact very knowledgeable about music. For Barbara is not solely responsible for my recovery of the assumption in (19).

As we have seen, a speaker's decision to convey information implicitly rather than explicitly is governed by his assessment of the hearer's contextual resources. A speaker who does expect his utterance to be interpreted in a particular way must assume that the contextual assumptions required for the recovery of this interpretation are immediately accessible. In some cases the speaker has grounds for thinking that the hearer will access the required assumptions of her own accord. For example, if I knew Simon and Jane had previously agreed that they would meet in Simon's office at 11 o'clock, it would be reasonable for me to assume that Jane will recover something like the assumption in (21) from the utterance in (20):

(20) It's after 11.
(21) I should be in Simon's office by now.

As we saw in chapter 1, it is not that the speaker and hearer share the required contextual assumption in advance of the utterance, but rather that the speaker has reasonable confidence that the hearer will be able to access the required information upon hearing his utterance. Recall the example (taken from Sperber and Wilson) in which Mary and Peter are looking at a landscape in which Mary has noticed a distant church. That Peter has not already noticed that the building is a church does not mean that he will not be able to understand Mary's utterance in (22).

(22) I've been inside that church.

All that is necessary is that Peter is able to identify the building as a church when required to.

In both these examples, then, the speaker had fairly specific expectations about the way in which his utterance would be interpreted, but assumed that the hearer would recover the intended interpretation of her own accord. There was no need for her to make it clear that this was the interpretation she intended. In other words, there was no need for Mary to constrain Peter's interpretation in any way.

In contrast, the speaker of the indirect answer in (3) (repeated below) forces the hearer to access the contextual assumption in (5) and to derive the contextual implication in (4).

(3) A: Did I get invited to the conference?
      B: Your paper was too long.
(5) If your paper is too long for the conference you will not be invited.
(4) Speaker A did not get invited to the conference.

For as we have seen, this is the only way for the hearer to maintain her assumption that the utterance was consistent with the principle of relevance.

This suggests that speakers make decisions not only about whether what they want to communicate is to be explicated or implicated, but also about the extent to which they will constrain the hearer's recovery of implicatures. Clearly, this decision too will be affected by the speaker's estimation of the hearer's contextual and processing resources. In this section we have considered cases in which the speaker constrains the hearer's interpretation by exploiting her assumption that the utterance is consistent with the principle of relevance. That is, the constraint is a purely pragmatic (or non-linguistic) one. In chapter 8 we shall consider a number of ways in which the speaker may use the linguistic form of his utterance to constrain the hearer's choice of context and thus the implicatures she recovers. Our concern with constraints on implicatures inevitably means a concern with relatively strong implicatures. However, we shall be returning to weak implicatures in chapter 9 when we turn our attention to questions about poetry and style.

Exercise 1

1 Grice (1975) analyses certain implicatures as arising from the violation of a maxim. In some cases, he claims, the violation can be explained by the assumption that the maxim clashes with another. For example, given the contextual assumption that A wants to see his friend C, B can be taken to be implicating the assumption in (b).

> (a) A: Where does C live?
>   B: Somewhere in the south of France.
> (b) B does not know in which town C lives.

According to Grice, B's answer is less informative than is required to meet A's needs. However, he suggests this can be explained in terms of the supposition that B is aware that to give more information would be to infringe another maxim – 'Don't say what you lack adequate evidence for.'

Sperber and Wilson's Relevance Theory has only one pragmatic principle, and hence there is no possibility of clashes. How would you account for the interpretation of B's utterance in (a) in this framework? Do you need to appeal to the *violation* of a pragmatic principle?

2 Grice claims that in other examples of implicature a maxim may appear to violated at the level of what is said, but the hearer is entitled to assume that that maxim (or at least the Co-operative Principle) is obeyed at the level of what is implicated. Consider his example of a professor who provides (a) as a testimonial for a pupil who is a candidate for a job in a Philosophy department.

> (a) Dear Sir, Mr X's command of English is excellent, and his attendance at tutorials has been regular. Yours etc.

Grice claims that the implicature in (b) arises because the professor is deliberately flouting the maxim which requires him to give sufficient information: the professor clearly has more information than this, and he knows that more information is required. He must therefore be wishing to convey information which he is reluctant to write down.

> (b) Mr X is no good at Philosophy.

How would you analyse this example in Sperber and Wilson's framework (that is, without appealing to the deliberate violation of a pragmatic principle)?

Recommended Reading

Grice's Theory of Conversational Implicature

Grice 1975: 41–58; 1989: 22–40.
Levinson 1983: 100–18.
Leech 1983: 30–44 (a socio-cultural interpretation of Grice).

Implicated Assumptions and Implicated Conclusions

Sperber and Wilson 1986: 133–7, 193–202.
Wilson and Sperber 1986.

The Strength of Implicatures

Sperber and Wilson 1986: 56–7, 197–206, 221–2.
Grice 1975: 58.

Note

1 For example, proponents of the mutual-knowledge approach to the context. See section 2.3 for a more detailed discussion of this point.

8 Constraints on Implicatures

8.1 Connections in Discourse

In chapter 5 we saw that the notion of textual coherence can be explained in terms of the principle of relevance. Given the hearer's assumption that the speaker has aimed at optimal relevance, it is not surprising that she will assume that an utterance which is part of a text or discourse can be interpreted as somehow following on from the preceding utterances. Thus, for example, in (1) the interpretation of the first segment provides an immediately accessible context for the recovery of the enriched proposition in (2).

(1) David got on the horse. He rode away.
(2) David$_i$ got on [the horse]$_j$ at t$_n$ He$_i$ rode away on [the horse]$_j$ at t$_{n+1}$

This is an example in which the interpretation of the first segment gives the hearer access to a context which enables her to recover the proposition expressed by the following segment. As we have seen, utterance interpretation is not simply a matter of identifying the proposition expressed. It is also a matter of recovering the intended contextual effects of the utterance. It is not surprising, then, that the coherence of a text or discourse may derive from the fact that one segment gives the hearer access to a context which enables her to derive the intended contextual effects from the next. In other words, the coherence of a text may derive from the way in which the relevance of one segment depends on the interpretation of another.

For example, in the sequence in (3) the second segment will be understood as being connected to the first by virtue of being an explanation for the state of affairs it describes, or in other words, by virtue of being an answer to a question – Why? – which is raised by the presentation of the first segment.

(3) David cut his finger. The knife slipped.

Since questions and answers are by their very nature planned as distinct utterances each satisfying the principle of relevance individually, it is not surprising that this kind of connection cannot be expressed by a conjoined utterance, where only the relevance of the conjoined proposition as a whole is guaranteed under the principle of relevance. Thus although (4) may be acceptable in certain contexts, the second conjunct cannot be interpreted as an explanation for the state of affairs described in the first.

(4)   David cut his finger and the knife slipped.

Of course, the second segment of (3) is only an explanation for the state of affairs described in the first segment given a contextual assumption along the lines of the one in (5).

(5)   Letting a knife slip can cause the user to cut himself.

In other words, the hearer can establish this particular connection only by supplying particular contextual assumptions.

Obviously, this is not the only way in which the relevance of an utterance may depend on the interpretation of the preceding text. As we have seen in chapter 2, there are three ways in which a new item of information may be relevant. First, it may allow the derivation of a contextual implication. Second, it may provide further evidence for and hence strengthen an existing assumption. And third, it may contradict an existing assumption and lead to the elimination of an assumption. In each case establishing the relevance of a new assumption involves inference. And in each case it depends on the contextual assumptions that are brought to bear.

For example, given the contextual assumption in (6), the information in (7) will be relevant in virtue of yielding the contextual implication in (8).

(6)   If David isn't here, then Barbara is in town.
(7)   David isn't here.
(8)   Barbara is in town.

Given the assumptions in (9), then the information in (7) will be relevant in virtue of providing further evidence for the assumption in (9a).

(9)   (a)   We shall have to cancel the meeting.
      (b)   If David isn't here, we shall have to cancel the meeting.

And given the assumptions in (10), the information in (7) will be relevant in virtue of contradicting and eliminating an existing assumption (namely, the weaker of the two assumptions that led to the contradiction).

(10)   (a)   If Barbara is in town, then David will be here.
       (b)   Barbara is in town.

In the light of this consider the sequence in (11). (For the purposes of this discussion it is not important whether or not both segments are uttered by the same speaker.)

(11)   (a)   Barbara is in town.
       (b)   David isn't here.

According to the arguments so far, the interpretation of segment (a) should provide the hearer with an immediately accessible assumption for the interpretation of segment (b). The problem is that in principle the utterance in (11a) may give the hearer access to all sorts of contextual assumptions, and it may not be clear which assumptions the hearer is intended to bring to bear on the interpretation of the utterance in (11b). In other words, it may not be clear just how (11b) is intended to be interpreted in the context of (11a).

For example, (11b) may be relevant as something that the hearer is trying to prove by presenting the assumption in (11a). It may be relevant by making explicit an intended contextual effect of (11a). It may be relevant as evidence for the claim in (11a). It may be relevant by providing further evidence for an assumption that has been derived from (11a). Or it may be relevant in virtue of contradicting and eliminating an assumption that has been derived from (11a).

In actual discourse the connection between the two utterances would not be left unspecified, and the speaker would constrain the interpretation of (11b) either by intonation or by the use of *discourse connectives* like *so, after all, moreover,* or *however.* Consider the differences between the following:

(12)   Barbara isn't in town. So David isn't here.
(13)   Barbara isn't in town. After all, David isn't here.
(14)   Barbara isn't in town. Moreover, David isn't here.
(15)   Barbara isn't in town. However, David isn't here.

8.2   Discourse Connectives as Constraints on Implicatures

Notice that in order to establish the connection prescribed by *so* or *after all* the hearer must supply the contextual assumption in (16).[1]

(16)   Whenever David isn't here Barbara is in town.

However, whereas the speaker of (12) is suggesting that the hearer did not already know that David isn't here, the speaker of (13) is suggesting that this is something the hearer already knows. This means that the use of *after all*, in contrast with the use of *so*, indicates that the utterance it introduces is relevant as a reminder. Hence the suggestion in (13) that the hearer should have also known that Barbara was in town.

According to the definition developed in chapter 7, the *implicatures* of an utterance include those contextual assumptions which the hearer has to supply in order to preserve her assumption that the utterance is consistent with the principle of relevance. As we have seen, the hearer's choice of utterance sometimes leaves the hearer with very little option as to the contextual assumptions she brings to bear. (Recall here indirect answers.) We may say that these are cases in which the speaker imposes constraints on the implicatures of the utterance. Now we have also seen how a speaker may use a linguistic expression to indicate how the utterance it introduces is to be interpreted as relevant. Since the hearer is forced to supply particular contextual assumptions in order to interpret the utterance in accordance with the meaning of such an expression, these expressions must be regarded as imposing constraints on implicatures.

The idea that there are linguistic constructions which impose constraints on the contexts in which utterances containing them can occur was proposed by Stalnaker (1974).[2] However, in the absence of an adequate account of the selection and use of the context in utterance interpretation it was not clear why such constructions should exist.

It should by now be clear that in a relevance-based framework the existence of these constructions is not surprising. According to this framework, hearers interpret every utterance in the smallest and most accessible context that yields adequate contextual effects for no unjustifiable effort. This means that if a speaker wishes to constrain the interpretation recovered by a hearer, he must constrain the hearer's choice of context. And since the constructions we are considering ensure correct context selection at minimal processing cost, they can be regarded as effective means for constraining the interpretation of utterances in accordance with the principle of relevance.

8.3   The Classification of Discourse Connectives

In fact, it seems that this framework allows us to make a more specific claim about the relationship between linguistic structure and pragmatic interpretation. According to section 8.1, there are three ways in which information conveyed by an utterance can be relevant:

1   It may allow the derivation of a contextual implication.
2   It may strengthen an existing assumption (by providing better evidence
    for it).
3   It may contradict an existing assumption.

As we have seen, one major way in which an utterance may achieve contextual
effect is by answering a question raised by the interpretation of the previous
utterance. However, a hearer is entitled to expect that she can obtain some sort
of contextual effect whether the utterance is part of a text/discourse or not.
Moreover, even when an utterance is part of a text/discourse it is not always
processed for relevance in a context provided by the interpretation of the
previous utterance. Recall the example given in section 5.3, where B's response
can be construed either as a report of an assertion made by Jane or as an
assertion by B that the bus is coming.

(17)   A: What did Jane say?
       B: The bus is coming.

However, if the hearer *does* interpret an utterance in the context of the
interpretation of the preceding text, then it follows that it will be connected to
that text in one of the three ways corresponding to 1–3 above. It also follows
that a language may develop structures which constrain the hearer's interpretation in any of the three ways corresponding to 1–3, or, in other words, three
types of discourse connective. As we shall see in section 8.4, this is not an
exhaustive classification: for instance, there are expressions which indicate the
role of the utterance in the discourse in which it occurs (for example, *anyway*,
incidentally, by the way, finally), and there are also expressions which indicate
what *kind* of contextual implications the hearer is expected to derive.[3] We
shall be considering some of these expressions in the following section.
However, in the mean time let us concentrate on the broad classification just
outlined.

Discourse Connectives which Introduce Contextual Implications

So far our discussion of discourse connectives has been restricted to the cases in
which an expression is used to indicate how the utterance it introduces is
relevant in a context which is made accessible by the interpretation of the
preceding utterance. However, many of these so-called 'connectives' can be
used to constrain the interpretation of an utterance even though they are not

used to connect two segments of text. The role of *so* in (18) is exactly the same as its role in (19).

(18)   A: You take the first turning on the left.
       B: So we don't go past the university (then).

(19)   (*Hearer (who is driving) makes a left turn*)
       So we're not going past the university (then/after all).[4]

In both cases the speaker is confirming that the proposition *so* introduces is indeed a contextual implication of an assumption which has been made accessible. Whereas in (18) this assumption is made accessible by another utterance, in (19) the speaker is drawing attention to an assumption that he has derived from his observation of an event.

   This use of *so* is clearly related to the one in (20) where the speaker is asking A what the intended relevance of her utterance is.

(20)   A: Your clothes smell of perfume.
       B: So (what)?

B is, of course, asking (rhetorically) what conclusion is he is expected to draw. A proposition that is introduced by *so* must be interpreted as a conclusion. The same point can, of course, be made about *therefore*. However, while *so* can be used as a (more informal) substitute for *therefore*, it seems that *therefore* cannot always be substituted for *so*. Thus while both *so* and *therefore* are acceptable in (21), the use of *therefore* is unacceptable in examples like (19) and (20).

(21)   This suggestion can be cancelled without contradiction. Therefore/So it
       is an implicature.

(22)   (Hearer arrives laden with parcels)
       ?Therefore you've spent all your money?

(23)   A: Your clothes smell of perfume.
       ?B: Therefore (what)?

Whereas in (21) *so* is being used to introduce a proposition that the speaker is aiming to *prove* by the presentation of another, in (18) to (20) it is not. That this use of *so* (and *therefore*) must be preceded by another utterance is not surprising in view of the fact, first, that an assumption may provide proof only if it comes with a guarantee of factuality, and, second, that only communicated assumptions come with any sort of guarantee of relevance. In other words, a speaker can't be said to be *proving* something if he doesn't present the proof.[5]

Discourse Connectives concerned with Strengthening

Of course speakers do not always present the proof and then the conclusion. As we have seen, the use of *after all* indicates that the proposition it introduces is evidence for an assumption which has just been made accessible. In (24) the proposition introduced by *after all* is relevant as justification for the claim in the first utterance of the sequence.

(24)   You have to have another drink. After all it is your birthday.

In other words, the aim is to increase the strength of the hearer's commitment to the assumption conveyed in the first utterance.

The aim is rather similar in (25), except here speaker B is providing *additional* evidence for an assumption which is derived from the first segment.

(25)   A: Will you make pancakes?
       B: I haven't really got time tonight. Besides there's no milk.

The suggestion is that the hearer is expected to derive the conclusion in (26) from the proposition expressed by the first utterance *and* from the proposition expressed by the second utterance.

(26)   B will not make pancakes.

Since a conclusion that is derived from two separate sets of premises will inherit a degree of strength greater than the one that it inherits from either set alone, the effect of presenting the additional evidence is to strengthen the guarantee that the speaker is offering for the factuality of (26) in his first utterance. Other expressions which introduce additional evidence are *moreover, furthermore* and utterance-initial *also*.[6]

These are not, however, the only expressions which have to do with the strengthening of existing assumptions. In (27) B's use of *indeed* indicates that his utterance is relevant as confirmation of the assumption conveyed by A's utterance.[7]

(27)   A: That's good news.
       B: It is, indeed.

This kind of utterance stands in direct contrast to the type we shall consider next, where the speaker's intention is to contradict some element of the interpretation of a preceding utterance.

Discourse Connectives which Introduce Denials

Consider the exchange in (28) where B's intention is to *deny* the assumption conveyed in the preceding utterance.

(28)   A: David isn't here.
       B: Yes he is.

As we have seen, a hearer who is presented with an assumption which is inconsistent with an existing one will abandon the one for which she has the least evidence. This means that an utterance may be relevant in virtue of providing evidence for an assumption which is inconsistent with an assumption which the speaker believes the hearer to hold. In (28) the speaker simply presents a proposition which is inconsistent with the one expressed by A's utterance, and the hearer will abandon her assumption only if she thinks that B has better evidence than she has. In (29) speaker B presents evidence for the truth of a proposition which is inconsistent with the one expressed by A's utterance, and the effect will depend on just how good the hearer thinks this evidence is.

(29)   A: David isn't here.
       B: I just saw him in his office.

In these examples there is no need for the speaker to indicate how he expects his utterance to be interpreted. However, there are cases in which the speaker must indicate that his utterance is relevant as a denial. In (30), for example, the use of *however* indicates that the proposition it introduces is inconsistent with a proposition that the speaker assumes the hearer has derived as a contextual implication from the first utterance.

(30)   David is here. However, you can't see him.

This means that the speaker's use of *however* is appropriate only if he assumes that the speaker has immediate access to contextual assumptions which allow the derivation of the implication that the hearer can see David. And this, of course, is not necessarily the case – the hearer might have brought quite different contextual assumptions to bear and derived quite different contextual implications. The use of *however* indicates how the speaker thought the hearer would have interpreted the first utterance.

There are a number of other expressions that play this sort of role, for example *still*, *nevertheless* and, most notoriously, *but*.[8] Evidently, these are not completely interchangeable in all contexts. That is, they do not impose exactly the same constraint. However, I shall have to leave it to the reader to identify the precise nature of the differences between these expressions.

8.4   Parallel Implications

As we saw in section 8.3, a speaker may intend to achieve relevance by contradicting (and thus eliminating) an assumption communicated by the previous utterance. Now, it is possible that B's utterance in (31) is relevant in this way.

(31)   A: Jane has a laser printer.
       B: Simon has a laser printer.

However, it will be recognized that there is another possibility, namely, that B is simply intending to give some additional information that is relevant in the same way as the information that was presented by A. In other words, B might have been intending the hearer to derive contextual effects *parallel* to the ones that she has derived from A.

In (31) this parallelism is suggested by the parallelism of the syntax. Similarly, in (32) the parallelism in structure encourages the hearer to derive parallel implicatures – hence the amusing effect.[9]

(32)   Mary came with Peter, Joan with Bob, and Lily with a sad smile on her face. (from Sperber and Wilson (1987))

However, there are linguistic expressions that can be used to make the speaker's intentions more explicit. Thus B might have responded to A with either (33a) or (33b).

(32)   (a)   Simon has also got a laser printer.
       (b)   Simon's got a laser printer too.

The use of *too* and *also* indicates that the utterance should be processed in such a way as to yield the same sort of contextual effects as were derived from the previous utterance.[10]

As the following examples show, both *too* and *also* interact with the phenomenon known as *focus*. (Capitals indicate heavy stress.)

(34) (a) Simon cooked a chicken. He also cooked a DUCK.
      (b) Simon bought a chicken. He also COOKED one.
      (c) Jane cooked a chicken. Simon ALSO cooked one.

The speaker of (34a) will be understood as having taken (35a) for granted, the speaker of (34b) will be understood as having taken (35b) for granted, and the speaker of (34c) will be understood as taking (35c) for granted.

(35) (a) Simon cooked something else.
      (b) Simon did something else with a chicken.
      (c) Someone else cooked a chicken.

The values of the variables *something else* and *someone else* are, of course, given in the first utterance of the sequence.

The differences in interpretation are due to a different constituent being focused in each case.. Let us consider this phenomenon in isolation from the meaning of *also*.[11]

Each of the following expresses the same proposition – namely that Simon cooked a chicken. However, they convey this information in different ways.

(36) (a) It was Simon who cooked a chicken.
      (b) It was a chicken that Simon cooked.

While both (36a) and (36b) entail the propositions in (37), the speaker of (36a) will be understood as having taken (37a) but not (37b) for granted, while the speaker of (36b) will be understood as having taken (37b) but not (37a) for granted:

(37) (a) Someone cooked a chicken.
      (b) Simon cooked something.

Wilson and Sperber (1979) would analyse the difference between these two utterances in terms of the way they are interpreted as relevant. Whereas the main relevance of the utterance in (36a) derives from the identity of the person who cooked the chicken, the main relevance of (36b) derives from the identity of the thing that was cooked. Since the relevance of an assumption depends on the contextual assumptions that are brought to bear on its interpretation, this means that the difference between these utterances must be due to their being processed in different contexts.

As we have seen, both (36a) and (36b) entail the propositions in (37a) and (37b). These entailments are obtained by substituting a variable for a grammatical constituent. Hence Wilson and Sperber's term *grammatically specified entailments*. Other grammatically specified entailments of (36a) and (36b) are given below:

(37)   (c)   Simon did something with a chicken.
       (d)   Simon did something.

Their first point is that although a speaker who expresses the proposition in (38) will have committed himself to the truth of all these entailments, he will not expect them all to play the same role in establishing the relevance of his utterance.

(38)   Simon cooked a chicken.

In their terms, the relevance of the utterance will depend on which of these entailments is taken as *background*. If, for example, (37a) is taken as background, then the hearer will process the utterance in a context in which it would be relevant to know the identity of the person who cooked a chicken. If, on the other hand, (37b) is taken as background, then the utterance will be processed in a context in which it would be relevant to know what Simon cooked. The point or main relevance of the utterance derives from information that has to be added to the background to obtain the proposition as a whole.

How does the hearer know which entailment she is expected to take as background? As the examples in (36a) and (36b) show, there are linguistic devices which serve to highlight a constituent so that it is understood to be part of the point of the utterance. In contrast, a speaker who presents information in a parenthetical clause, as for example in (39), will indicate that this is not part of the main point of the utterance.

(39)   Simon, who is a mathematician, cooked a chicken.

As Wilson and Sperber point out, these syntactic devices affect pragmatic interpretation only through their interaction with stress assignment. Thus for example, the heavy stress on *cooked* in (40) indicates that the background is the entailment in (37c).

(40)　Simon COOKED a chicken.

On the other hand, normal stress is ambivalent in its contribution to utterance interpretation and does not determine a unique focus. Thus a speaker who places focal stress on *chicken* in (41) may be using it to focus on any of the constituents that contain it – for example, the NP *a chicken*, the VP *bought a chicken*, or the entire S.

(41)　Simon cooked a chicken.

Evidently, some account has to be given of how the actual focus is chosen from a range of possible foci. However, this would take us beyond the scope of this section of the book, which is not concerned with stress and focus in themselves, but with expressions which interact with focal stress to impose a particular constraint on the interpretation of the utterances that contain it.

As we have seen, the use of *also* indicates that the hearer is expected to derive implicatures parallel to the ones she has derived from the previous utterance. We have also seen that contrastive stress serves to highlight a constituent so that it will be understood as contributing to the point of the utterance. This means that in (34b) (repeated here as (42)) the speaker expects the hearer to process the second segment in a context in which (a) it is relevant to know what Simon did with a chicken, and (b) the contextual effects of knowing what Simon did with a chicken are parallel to the ones derived from knowing that Simon did something else with a chicken. As I have pointed out, the hearer is told what else Simon did with a chicken in the preceding segment.

(42)　Simon bought a chicken. He also COOKED a chicken.

In contrast, the hearer of (43) is not informed as to what Simon did with a chicken in the first segment. Hence the unacceptability of the sequence as a whole.

(43)　Jane cooked a chicken. Simon also COOKED a chicken.

Exercise 1

1　It is generally recognized that the use of *but* mentioned above (section 8.3) must be distinguished from the uses illustrated in (a) to (c).

(a)　David is in but Nigel is out.
(b)　Jane is tall but Anne is short.
(c)　Simon eats wholefood but Tom eats at McDonald's.

In these uses (which are distinguished from the one discussed above by being symmetric) *but* is said to have a *contrastive* function. To what extent do you think this use can be analysed in terms of parallel implicature?

Note the characteristic intonation pattern associated with this use of *but*.

David is ˇ in but Nigel is ˋ out.

For further reading see Blakemore (1987: 125–41; 1989) and R. Lakoff (1971).

2 Discuss the contribution made to the interpretation of the following text by the italicised expressions and constructions. The reference is to an interview with Madonna conducted by Wogan, a British television chat-show host.

> *Well*, what do you ask the girl who has everything? Perhaps not, 'Have you met Andrew Lloyd Webber', as Wogan did, *but* clearly the man was *out of his familiar studio, out of his depth, and in a very strange shirt.* Maybe it was not fair to expect anything more raunchy or, *indeed*, relevant from Wogan; *after all*, it was early evening on the BBC. (*Guardian*, 30 July 1990)

Note: For two very different analyses of *well*, see Schiffrin (1985b) and Carlson (1984).

8.5 Non-Truth-Conditional Meaning: Semantics and Pragmatics

Some of the expressions and constructions we have been examining, for example *after all* and *moreover*, have received relatively little attention in the literature on semantics and pragmatics. Others, for example *but*, *too*, and focusing devices (like contrastive stress and clefting), have gained a certain notoriety. This notoriety derives from a property which is shared by virtually all the expressions we have been considering (including *after all* and *moreover*) – namely, that they do not contribute towards the *truth conditions* of the utterances that contain them. In other words, they are counter-examples to the view that all meaning can be analysed in truth-conditional terms. Thus, to take one of the more notorious examples, it is generally agreed that (44a) and (44b) are true under the same conditions – namely, when Nigel is home and he is busy. A hearer who was unable to interpret the second conjunct of (44a) as denying an expectation created by the interpretation of the first conjunct would not accuse the speaker of speaking *falsely*.

(44) (a) Nigel is home but he's busy.
      (b) Nigel is home and he is busy.

Similarly, to take another notorious example, it is generally agreed that both (45a) and (45b) are true if and only if David kissed Barbara.

(45) (a) It was David who kissed Barbara.
      (b) It was Barbara whom David kissed.

Yet as we have seen, they will have very different interpretations.

It seems that Grice (1975), who first introduced the term *implicature*, used it to refer to any aspect of meaning that could not be analysed in truth-conditional terms. A *conversational implicature* was a proposition which was derived from an utterance on the basis of the meanings of the words uttered, the context and the assumption that the speaker had been speaking in accordance with a co-operative principle and certain maxims of conversation. Thus for example, on the assumption that the speaker was trying to be informative, the hearer of (46) will derive the assumption in (47).

(46) A: I've run out of petrol.
      B: There's a garage down the road.

(47) A can obtain petrol from the garage down the road.

As I have mentioned, the advantage of this approach was that it enabled Grice to provide a non-linguistic account of phenomena which had seemed to be problematic for a truth-conditional theory of semantics. For example, it seemed to provide a non-linguistic explanation for the non-truth-functional uses of the logical connectives (for example, *and* and *or*).[12] However, as Grice recognized, there are examples of non-truth-conditional meaning which cannot be analysed in non-linguistic terms. Thus the suggestion conveyed in (48), that his being brave is a consequence of his being an Englishman) is due to the meaning of *therefore*, and yet, according to Grice, the speaker could not be accused of speaking falsely should the consequence in question fail to hold.

(48) He is an Englishman. He is, therefore, brave.

Grice gives this as an example of *conventional implicature* – that is, an implicature which is not derived on the basis of the maxims of conversation, but which is encoded linguistically.

As we have seen, a number of linguists and philosophers have proposed that this notion could form the basis for an account of non-truth-conditional meaning (see Karttunen (1974) and Karttunen and Peters (1975)). The problem is that in introducing this notion Grice said no more than that conventional implicatures (like the one associated with *therefore*) did not contribute to truth conditions.

However, more recently Grice (1989) developed this notion further. His first example is the use of the contrastive expression *on the other hand* in (49).

(49)   My brother-in-law lives on a peak in Darien; his great aunt, on the other hand, was a nurse in World War I.

He says:

> Speakers may be at the one and the same time engaged in performing speech acts at different but related levels. One part of what [the speaker of (48)] is doing is making what might be called ground floor statements about the brother-in-law and his great aunt, but at the same time he is also performing a higher-order speech act of commenting in a certain way on the lower-order speech acts. (Grice 1989: 362)

Specifically, the speaker of (49) is performing a higher-level speech act of contrasting, and he indicates this by his use of *on the other hand*. The performance or misperformance of this higher-level act will not, claims Grice, affect the truth value of the speaker's words. The truth conditions of (49) are determined only by the lower-level act.

His second example of conventional implicature is the suggestion carried by *so*. He claims that in an example like the one in (50) the speaker is performing two speech acts, a lower-order one in which he communicates the propositions in (51), and a higher-order one in which he communicates the proposition in (52).

(50)   Our computer is down. So I can't help you.
(51)   (a)   The computer at the speaker's office is down.
       (b)   The speaker can't help the hearer.
(52)   The proposition in (51b) is an explanation for the state of affairs represented in (51a).

This analysis is reminiscent of the analysis proposed for performative expressions in chapter 6. It will be recalled that, according to this analysis, the utterance in (53) communicates two explicatures, the lower-level explicature in (54a) and the higher-level explicature in (54b).

(53) I warn you that the roads are icy.
(54) (a) The roads are icy.
      (b) The speaker of (53) is warning the hearer that the roads are icy.

The main relevance of the utterance generally lies in (54a) rather than in (54b). Moreover, it has often been claimed that in this sort of example the truth value of the utterance depends only on the state of affairs represented in (54a). The function of the higher-order proposition is to constrain the interpretation of the lower-order proposition so that the hearer is encouraged to derive certain sorts of implicatures (ones that have to do with the dangerous consequences of the state of affairs represented in (54a)).

Notice that according to this account, although the meaning of the performative expression does not contribute to the proposition expressed by the utterance and hence its truth conditions, it is analysed in *representational* terms. That is, while it does not contribute to the proposition expressed by the utterance, it does contribute to a propositional representation. The question is whether we can analyse all examples of non-truth-conditional meaning in this way.[13] In particular, the question is whether we can analyse all Grice's examples of conventional implicature in this way, as Grice himself seems to have intended.

What other way is there? Recall that according to the relevance-theoretic framework adopted in this book, understanding utterances involves the construction of mental (propositional) representations which undergo inferential computations. That is, establishing the relevance of the proposition expressed by the second segment of (55) involves combining it with other (contextual) assumptions and making an inference.

(55) (a) David isn't here.
      (b) Barbara's in town.

Now, it is generally accepted that linguistic meaning plays a role in the identification of the propositional representations that are manipulated in these computations – in, for example, the identification of the proposition that Barbara is in town.[14] But given that these representations are intended to undergo mental computations – to act as premises in deductions – it is surely possible that linguistic meaning also plays a role in determining *how* they are to be manipulated. In other words, it is possible that some linguistic meaning is *procedural* rather than representational.

This is the idea underlying the analysis of expressions like *so*, *after all*, *however* and *moreover* in section 8.3 above. According to this analysis, the hearer of a sequence like (55) could be instructed to process the proposition expressed by (55b) in a particular kind of context – for example, in a context which enabled her to identify the proposition as a contextual effect of the preceding segment. Or she could be instructed to process it in a context which enabled her to identify the proposition as justification for the proposition expressed in the previous utterance. The first kind of instruction is given by *so*, while the second is given by *after all*.

This procedural analysis of *so* contrasts with Grice's representational one. It treats the speaker of (56) as instructing the hearer to interpret (56b) as a conclusion (a contextual implication), while Grice treats him as communicating the information that (56a) is an explanation.

(56) (a)   David isn't here.
      (b)   So Barbara's in town.

However, while Grice's account might work in (56), it does not seem to work in cases where the utterance containing *so* is not preceded by another utterance. Recall the example given in section 8.3 in which the hearer enters the room laden with parcels and the speaker produces the utterance in (57).

(57)   So you've spent all your money.

Since there is no preceding utterance which can be interpreted as an explanation, the speaker cannot be explaining why the hearer has spent all her money. In contrast, in both (56) and (57) the utterance introduced by *so* can be interpreted as a conclusion.

If Grice's analysis is right, then there is a concept corresponding to *so*. However, while this may be the case for the ProVP *so*, and the manner adverbial *so*, it does not seem to be the case for the inferential *so* that we have been discussing here.[15] Moreover, it certainly does not seem to be the case for expressions like *moreover, after all*, or *however*.[16]

According to standard speech-act analyses, performatives like *I warn* and *I predict* do not contribute to the truth conditions of the utterances that contain them.[17] However, as has been shown in chapter 6, these expressions must be analysed in representational terms. In particular, they contribute towards a proposition whose relevance lies in the way it directs the hearer towards a particular interpretation of another proposition. In other words, some linguistic meaning is representational but non-truth-conditional.

But now we have also seen that there are expressions whose meanings cannot be analysed in representational terms at all. *But, after all, moreover* and inferential *so* do not contribute to a propositional representation, but simply encode instructions for processing propositional representations. The existence of non-truth-conditional meaning has led linguists and philosophers to realize that there may not after all be a unitary theory of linguistic semantics. However, the point is not simply that linguistic meaning may be either truth-conditional or non-truth-conditional. It may also be either representational or procedural. That there can be these different types of meaning is not surprising given the nature of the processes involved in understanding utterances and the nature of the principle governing those processes.

Recommended Reading

Connections in Discourse: Relevance-Theoretic Approaches

Blass 1990: 72–91.
Blakemore 1987: 105–131; 1988

Connections in Discourse: Other Approaches

Brown and Yule 1983: 223–6.
Halliday and Hasan 1976: chs 1 and 7.
van Dijk 1977: 1–11, 86–90.

Discourse Connectives

Blakemore 1987: 72–141.
Blass 1990: ch. 4.
Grice 1975: 44 (*therefore*).
Karttunen and Peters 1975 (a formal analysis of conventional implicature).

Parallel Implications

Wilson and Sperber 1979.
Sperber and Wilson 1986: 202–17.
Blass 1990: 134–56.

Non-Truth-Conditional Meaning

Grice 1975: 44; 1989: 359–65.
Karttunen and Peters 1975.
Wilson and Sperber 1990.

Notes

1 The ideas in sections 8.2 to 8.5 are based on those developed in Blakemore (1987).
2 Stalnaker refers to this phenomenon as *pragmatic presupposition*. Karttunen (1974) and Karttunen and Peters (1975) link this notion to Grice's (1975) notion of *conventional implicature*. However, their account, like Stalnaker's, raises the question of why such structures should exist. See Blakemore (1987) for a more detailed commentary.
3 We have already seen an example of such an expression – namely, the performative expression *I warn* (see section 6.2) which indicates that the hearer is expected to derive implications which have to do with the dangerous or unpleasant consequences of the state of affairs represented in the proposition it introduces.

   The discussion that follows is very brief. For more detailed analyses see Blakemore (1987).
4 Note that this utterance-final use of *after all* must be distinguished from the utterance-initial use discussed earlier.
5 See section 8.5 for further discussion of *therefore*.
6 See section 8.4 for discussion of *also* in its non-utterance-inital use.
7 Blass (1990) proposes that the so-called 'modal' use of the German expression *auch* can be analysed in terms of backwards confirmation, for example:

   A: Deine Schuhe sind genau richtig fur Dieses Wetter.
       Your shoes are just right for this weather.
   B: Sind sie auch.
       Indeed they are.

As she notes, in this kind of case, the speaker is confirming an explicature of the previous utterance. However, she also gives examples in which a speaker may use *auch* to indicatte that he is confirming an implicature.

   This is not, however, the only use of *auch*. Consider Blass's example:

   Klaus hat funf Autos und auch eine Jacht.
   Klaus has five cars and also a yacht.

Blass analyses this use in terms of *parallel processing* (see section 8.4). English is unlike German in that *also* cannot be used for backwards confirmation. However, Blass notes that there are other languages, for example, Sissala (a Niger-Congo language) which have expressions that can perform both functions.
8 Part of the notoriety of *but* derives from the fact that it is not always used in this way. R. Lakoff (1971) distinguishes between an asymmetric *denial of expectation but*, which corresponds to the use of *however* discussed here, and a symmetric *semantic contrast but* which is exemplified in

   Tom is short but Ben is short

For further discussion of this use see section 8.4.
   A number of writers, for example Kempson (1975) and Dascal and Katriel (1977), have argued against the claim that *but* is ambiguous. However, little

progress has been made in formulating a description of its meaning that unites all its uses. See Blakemore (1987: 125–41; 1989) for a detailed examination of this point.

9   Linguists will recognize this sort of phenomenon as gapping, while rhetoricians will recognize it as zeugma. The interpretation of this type of utterance will be discussed in more detail in chapter 9.

10 As we have seen in n. 8, the German expression *auch* can play a similar role. However, in contrast with *too* and *also*, *auch* can also play a role in indicating backwards confirmation. See Blass (1990: 136–56) for further discussion.

11 This type of phenomenon has been discussed in the pragmatics and semantics literature in terms of a variety of distinctions – for example the distinction between given and new information, topic and comment, theme and rheme, presupposition and focus. The difficulties associated with these distinctions have been discussed fully by Sperber and Wilson (1986: 202, 217) and Reinhart (1983). Here it suffices to say that there are two main problems. First, it is difficult to give the criteria for identifying information as, for example, old or as topic. Second, none of the distinctions is accompanied by an adequate account of the role that each type of information plays in utterance interpretation.

12 But see the discussion of conjoined utterances in section 5.2.

13 Deirdre Wilson (1990) has argued that so-called sentence adverbials like *frankly* and *unfortunately* can be analysed in terms of higher-level explicatures. That is, they are representational (in that they contribute to a propositional representation) but non-truth-conditional (in the sense that they do not contribute to the proposition expressed by the utterance, and hence to the truth conditions of the utterance.

14 However, as we saw in chapter 5, the proposition expressed by an utterance is very rarely fully determined by its linguistic properties.

15 In Blakemore (1987) I discuss a further use of *so* – the *and so* which is equivalent to *and as a result*.

(a)   It started to rain and so we stopped the game.
(b)   It started to rain and as a result we stopped the game.

This use of *so*, in contrast with the inferential one, seems to contribute to truth conditions.

16 Deirdre Wilson (personal communication) has persuaded me that a representational analysis does work for *therefore*. That is, she has suggested that in (a) *therefore* contributes to the higher-level explicature (b).

(a)   He is an Englishman. He is, therefore, brave.
(b)   It is a consequence of his being an Englishman that he is brave.

On this analysis there is no essential difference between *therefore* and the adverbial *consequently*.

As Ruth Kempson (1975) pointed out, there are certain uses of *therefore* in which it contributes to truth conditions. If *therefore* does not contribute to the truth conditions of (c), for example, Mary will have won her suit for damages if and only of (1) Bill hit her and (2) she was covered in bruises. This is not right. Mary will have won her suit for damages only if (1) Bill hit her and (2) she was covered in bruises as a result of Bill's hitting her.

(c) If Bill hit Mary and therefore she was covered in bruises, she will have won her suit for damages.

Notice, however, that the use of *therefore* in (a) is parenthetical. As Wilson (personal communication) has pointed out, whereas non-parenthetical uses of sentence adverbials like *unfortunately* do contribute to the truth conditions of utterances in which they occur, parenthetical uses arguably do not. The use of *unfortunately* in (d) contributes only to the higher-level explicature in (e), without affecting the truth conditions of the utterance at all.

(d) He is, unfortunately, an Englishman.
(e) It is unfortunate that he is an Englishman.

17 Recanati (1987) argues against this position.

9 Implicatures and Style

9.1 Poetic Effects

In the last chapter we considered examples in which the use of linguistic parallelisms encouraged the hearer to find matching parallelisms in implicatures. Thus in Sperber and Wilson's example (repeated here as (1)) the use of gapping indicates that the hearer's task is to find a set of contextual assumptions in which the facts that Mary came with Peter, Joan with Bob, and Lily with a sad smile on her face have identical or directly contrasting implicatures.

(1) Mary came with Peter, Joan with Bob, and Lily with a sad smile on her face.

However, although the linguistic form of the utterance suggests a specific processing strategy to the hearer, this strategy may yield a variety of acceptable interpretations. For there is a whole range of ways in which the hearer could recover the required parallelisms. Is Lily sad because, in contrast with the others, she had no one to come with? Does Lily make a point of appearing alone and sad? Is Lily's sad smile as familiar as the sight of the other couples? Do the others have anything to do with Lily's sad smile? In other words, this strategy leaves the hearer with a great deal of the responsibility in the interpretation process.

It is not that the hearer has to decide *which* of a range of possible interpretations the speaker intended. Indeed, it seems that a hearer who interpreted (1) as conveying merely a specific proposition or set of propositions would miss out on much of its intended relevance. Consider, for example, a hearer who interpreted (1) as conveying merely the proposition in (2).

(2) Mary came with Peter, Joan came with Bob, but Lily had no one to come with.

It is not difficult to see that this does not capture the full meaning intended by the speaker of (1). However, it is rather more difficult to say what exactly it fails to capture. An impression? An attitude? But impressions and attitudes are very vague things.

A similar problem arises in the case of (3) (repeated from chapter 6). The paraphrase in (4) does indicate the writer's attitude towards Joseph Sedley. Nevertheless, it misses out on something essential.

(3)   Being an invalid, Joseph Sedley contented himself with a bottle of claret besides his Madeira before dinner, and he managed a couple of plates full of strawberries and cream, and twenty four little rout cakes that were lying neglected in a plate near him. (Thackeray, *Vanity Fair*)

(4)   Joseph Sedley, who claimed to be a invalid, gorged himself on claret, strawberries and cream, and twenty four little rout cakes.

What is missing here? Some readers would say that (4) lacks the *bite* of the original. But what precisely is *bite*?

Whatever it is, it is surely not just decoration. It is not something that sits on top of the message – it is part of the message. Hence the inadequacy of the paraphrase. But this suggests that a theory of utterance understanding must be able to account for something as vague as an impression or bite.

It is clear that such an account cannot be given by the traditional approach to communication, which assumes that the hearer's task in utterance understanding is to identify a proposition (or set of propositions) specifically intended by the speaker together with the speaker's attitude towards that proposition (or set of propositions). As we have seen, whatever is conveyed by (1) or (3) cannot be elucidated in terms of a specific proposition or propositional attitude.

At this point we might simply conclude that since we are dealing with something vague, our account cannot be formulated in precise terms. Thus we might speak of the *connotations* of (1) and (3). Or we might simply leave notions like *bite* unexplained.

However, we have seen in section 7.1 that the traditional approach to communication cannot be maintained. Some speakers do indeed produce utterances in the expectation that the hearer will recover a specific set of propositions. But a speaker may produce an utterance with no expectation at all about the way in which it will be understood. In between these two extremes there is a whole range of intermediate cases. For example, we considered examples in which the speaker may encourage a hearer to supply contextual assumptions of a certain type and thus to derive a certain type of conclusion, but not care which specific assumptions are supplied and which specific conclusions are derived. In other words, there may be a range of acceptable contexts and contextual effects for the hearer to choose from. The exact extent of the range will vary according to how tightly the speaker constrains the hearer's interpretation. A speaker who constrains the interpretation of his utterance so that the hearer takes very little responsibility in the choice of contextual assumptions and contextual effects is said by Sperber and Wilson to be engaging in *strong communication*. The greater the responsibility the hearer has in the selection of contextual assumptions and effects, the *weaker* the communication.

In both (1) and (3) the hearer is left with a great deal of the responsibility for interpretation. In (1) the hearer is constrained to the extent that she is encouraged to find a context in which the implicatures derived from each of the three conjuncts are either identical or in direct contrast. However, as we have seen, there are all sorts of ways in which a hearer could spell out the story behind Lily's sad smile, and the result is a wide range of *weak implicatures*. The speaker weakly implicates (weakly communicates) the full range. A hearer who decides that a specific implicature from within the range is actually true (rather than possibly true) must take some of the responsibility for herself.

We shall be looking at (2) in more detail in the following section. However, I think that it is possible on the basis of the discussion so far to see that it involves both strong and weak communication. On the one hand, it strongly implicates that the author believes that Joseph Sedley's claim to be an invalid is ridiculous, and that his behaviour indicates gluttony rather than ill-health. On the other hand, there is a whole range of weak implicatures that the hearer can derive from these assumptions. It is on the basis of the weak implicatures that the hearer will create for herself an idea of just how ridiculous Joseph Sedley's behaviour is. In other words, the bite derives from the array of weak implicatures communicated by the passage.

Sperber and Wilson suggest that the effect of an utterance which achieves most of its relevance through a wide array of weak implicatures can be termed a *poetic effect*. This is not to suggest that such effects can be achieved only by poets. We have all produced ironic or metaphorical utterances. You may not want to call these everyday figurative utterances poetry, but they exhibit the characteristics of indeterminacy and vagueness just the same. The speaker of (5) will not be understood to be conveying just the proposition in (6). There is a whole range of implicatures that the hearer may derive from this proposition.

(5)　(*Barbara has just insulted Nigel*)
　　NIGEL: Barbara's always so tactful.
(6)　Barbara is always very tactless.

And the effect of (7) is lost in the paraphrase given in (8).

(7)   My neighbour is a dragon.
(8)   My neighbour is very fierce.

I would not want to suggest that there is nothing at all to distinguish poetic utterances from the sort of examples in (5) and (7). We shall return to this point in section 9.4 when we discuss questions of style. In the mean time, let us consider the poetic effects of metaphor and ironic utterances in more detail.

Exercise 1

The following poem is taken from an anthology, *Talking to the Sun*, in which the poems are accompanied by works of art (paintings, photographs, photographs of sculptures). The editors also provide commentaries for many of the poems. The commentary for this poem and its accompanying picture are given below. To what extent does the commentary capture the poem? What about the picture? Do you think that pictures and metaphors have anything in common?

Sleeping on the Ceiling

It is so peaceful on the ceiling!
It is the Place de la Concorde.
The little crystal chandelier
is off, the fountain in the dark.
Not a soul is in the park.

Below, where the wallpaper is peeling
the Jardin des Plantes has locked its gates.
Those photographs are animals.
The mighty flowers and foliage rustle;
under the leaves the insects tunnel.

We must go under the wallpaper
to meet the insect gladiator,
to battle with a net and trident,
and leave the fountain and the square.
But oh, that we could sleep up there . . .

(Elizabeth Bishop)

Commentary: Sometimes, just before going to sleep, you may experience the odd sensation of being in between the room where you really are and the imaginary room of your dreams.

Untitled (Gelatin silver photograph, 1976) by Jerry Uelsmann. (The Metropolitan Museum of Art, New York. Purchase, Warner Communications Inc. Gift and matching funds from the National Endowment for the Arts, 1981.)

9.2   Metaphor

Whatever the commentary represents, it does not represent *the* meaning of the poem. But nor does the picture, of course. For it, too, gives rise to a whole array of impressions and connotations. This might seem to suggest that the untranslatableness of metaphorical utterances means that their analysis is condemned to vagueness. In other words, it might seem that there is no way of analysing the impressions and connotations conveyed by a metaphorical utterance except in metaphorical terms. This, essentially, is the Romantic view described earlier in chapter 3.

The idea that we cannot paraphrase a picture is a familiar one. We may be led to notice things by a picture, a great many things. But there is no sense in which we can make an exhaustive list of them. As Davidson says, 'A picture is not worth a thousand words, or any other number. Words are the wrong currency to exchange for a picture' (1979: 45). His point is that metaphors are like pictures in this respect. They cause us to notice things, or, more specifically, to see things in a new light – much in the same way as a bump on the head or a drug. The problem is, according to Davidson, that there is no limit to what they can cause us to see, and much of what they cause us to notice is not propositional in nature.

According to this account, there is no point in asking what a metaphorical utterance *means*. The utterance in (7), for example, simply *means* that the speaker's neighbour is a dragon. That is, it simply means what the words mean in their literal interpretation. However, there *is* a point in asking what a metaphor *does*. The answer to this question hinges on an understanding of what it is to see something in a new light. Davidson says that this is the work of the imagination. Hence his claim, cited earlier, that metaphor is the dream-work of language.

If Davidson is right, then metaphorical utterances are distinguished from ordinary non-metaphorical utterances not by the fact that they convey a meaning which is not the one associated with the literal meanings of the words uttered, but by the fact that they are interpreted by means of a different faculty. And this means that an account of metaphor hinges on something which we do not have – an account of the workings of the imagination.

However, Davidson has not noticed that metaphorical utterances have a property that is shared by many non-metaphorical utterances. They do not represent the state of affairs they describe. As we have seen, this has been taken to imply that the speaker of a metaphorical utterance must mean something other than its literal meaning. However, we have seen that this view cannot be maintained. Moreover, there are other examples of utterances which would not be regarded as metaphorical, but which do not represent the state of affairs they describe. Sperber and Wilson call these *loose uses* of language, and suggest that there is no discontinuity between them and characteristic examples of poetic metaphor.

The key to this account of metaphor lies in the notion of *interpretive resemblance* introduced in chapter 6. This notion is based on the claim that any object can be used to represent any other object which it resembles. The idea that pictures, diagrams and actions can be used in this way is familiar enough. However, philosophers and linguists have either failed to notice that utterances may represent in this way or have failed to appreciate the significance of the fact that they do. Paraphrases, translations and summaries are all familiar cases in which an utterance can be used to represent another utterance. However, Sperber and Wilson claim that, more generally, an utterance can be used to represent *any* representation which it resembles in content, whether this be a public representation like an utterance, or a private representation like a thought. In fact, they claim that *every* utterance is an interpretive representation of a thought – namely, the thought that the speaker wishes to communicate.

This is not to say, however, that the hearer is entitled to expect that the utterance provides a literal interpretation of the speaker's thought. It may be sufficient for the speaker to provide a less-than-literal interpretation of his thought. Indeed, a less-than-literal representation may be more appropriate on some occasions than a completely literal one.

As we have seen, an object may be used to represent another object which it resembles to some extent. It is not necessary that the two objects be identical, only that they resemble each other in certain respects. And a communicator who uses one object to represent another expects his audience to be able to identify the respects in which the resemblance holds. To use Sperber and Wilson's example, when I draw a map showing you how to get to my house, I do not expect you to walk across a piece of white paper past signs saying 'pub' and 'supermarket' to a place marked with a cross.

Similarly, an utterance is an interpretive representation of another representation to the extent that it resembles it in semantic and logical properties, and the hearer must be able to identify the degree of faithfulness that has been attempted. This raises the question which we discussed only briefly in chapter 6: What is the criterion by which a hearer judges the degree of resemblance between an utterance and the thought it interprets?

Recall the example, given in chapter 6, in which you have met a friend you haven't seen for years, and during the conversation she asks you how much you earn. In fact you earn £897.56 a month. However, your answer is the one in (9):

(9)   £900 a month.

Although this answer is strictly false, it is appropriate in the situation described. Indeed, given the situation it would be inappropriate to have given the strictly true answer. Why?

Let us consider what your nosey friend might have inferred from your strictly false answer in (9). It is not difficult to imagine a context in which she might derive the contextual implications in (10).

(10) (a) The speaker is not as successful as I am.
      (b) The speaker would not be able to afford to live in my house.
      (c) The speaker would not be able to afford to own my car.
      (d) The speaker would not be able to afford a holiday abroad each
           year.

It is also not very difficult to imagine that these sorts of contextual implications would make your utterance relevant enough to be worth your friend's attention. Since there was no more economical way of conveying these implications, the hearer is entitled to assume that the utterance is consistent with the principle of relevance, and hence that she is entitled to interpret the utterance in the way I have just outlined.

It is of course *possible* that a hearer could have been misled by your answer, and have derived the conclusion in (11).

(11) The speaker earns exactly £225 a week.

However, in the situation described there would be no reason for you to think that your friend would have to derive this conclusion in order to establish the relevance of your utterance. Recall that according to the criterion of consistency with the principle of relevance, the speaker should be taken to have intended to communicate enough contextual effects to make his utterance optimally relevant, *and no more*. Therefore there would be no reason in this situation for your friend to think that this is an assumption that you, the speaker, endorsed.

If you *had* given the strictly true answer, then it would not have been optimally relevant unless the extra processing effort it entailed was rewarded by some contextual effect. But it is difficult to imagine what this might be. In other words, the complexity of the answer which literally represents your thoughts makes it less than optimally relevant. On the other hand, the assumptions which you wish to convey (that is, the assumptions about your spending power and standard of living) are derivable from a more easily processed utterance. The fact that this is not a literal interpretation of your thoughts does not matter. For although it may imply assumptions which you do not wish to endorse, it has logical and contextual implications which you do. Provided that the hearer can be trusted to sort out which of the logical and contextual implications are ones that you do wish to endorse, the less-than-literal answer is the best way of communicating your thought.

In other words, an utterance resembles a thought to the extent that it shares the logical and contextual implications of that thought. In some cases the optimally relevant utterance may be one which very closely resembles the speaker's thought. In other cases, the optimally relevant utterance may be one which involves a looser resemblance. Let us see how this idea might be applied to the analysis of metaphorical utterances.

As we have seen, metaphors vary from the highly creative (see, for example, the poem in Exercise 1) to the highly standardized. The fact that standardized metaphors like the one in (7) (repeated below) are so regularly used makes them relatively cheap to process.

(7)   My neighbour is a dragon.

Most hearers will have immediate access to stereotypical assumptions about dragons (or about what people say about dragons) which yield implicatures such as those in (12).

(12)   (a)   The speaker's neighbour is fierce.
       (b)   The speaker's neighbour is unfriendly.

That there are other stereotypical assumptions about dragons which yield implications that the speaker of (7) would not wish to endorse – for example, the implication in (13) – means that (7) is a less than literal interpretation of the speaker's thought.

(13)   The speaker's neighbour has a long tail.

If this lack of literalness is to be justified, then the speaker must have intended to convey something more than what would have been conveyed by saying merely, 'My neighbour is very unfriendly and fierce.' In other words, the utterance must suggest some further line of thought if the extra processing cost resulting from the element of indirectness in the metaphor is to be justified. For example, the speaker might be taken to have in mind an image of fierceness or unfriendliness which is beyond most people's experience, and the hearer is encouraged to explore a range of other contextual implications having to do with the nature of the neighbour's unfriendliness, the behaviour that manifests it and perhaps the neighbour's appearance. These implicatures are obviously weaker than the ones in (12) in that the hearer must take a greater responsibility for their recovery. However, it is these weak implicatures which justify the speaker's utterance as the best means of representing his thoughts, and it is these implicatures which explain why even this rather standardized example of metaphor cannot be paraphrased without loss.

In the case of more creative metaphors the hearer is given a greater share of the responsibility for the interpretation. Thus in Emilia's speech in (14) (which was discussed in chapter 3) the hearer is expected to go beyond the immediate context, accessing a wide range of assumptions to obtain a wide range of very weak implicatures.

(14)   'Tis not a year or two but show us a man,
        They are all but stomachs and we all but food,
        They eat us hungerly, and when they are full,
        They belch us.
                                    (*Othello*, III. iv)

Since each hearer has different background knowledge and a different imagination, different hearers will arrive at different conclusions. Hence the feeling shared by many literary critics that 'no two readings can be said to be exactly the same' (Ray 1984: 2).

It is possible that the implicatures the hearer recovers may themselves be metaphorical and thus invite still further processing. As Sperber and Wilson say, 'the surprise or beauty of a successful creative metaphor lies in this extreme condensation, in the fact that a single expression which has itself been loosely used will determine a wide range of acceptable weak implicatures' (1985/6: 168).

Notice that according to this account metaphorical utterances are neither deviant, as is suggested by the classical account (outlined in chapter 3), nor interpreted by means of a special type of interpretive ability, as is suggested by Davidson's account. A metaphorical utterance is simply one means of optimizing relevance, and is in this sense the consequence of very general abilities used in verbal commmunication. However, as we have seen, this is not to suggest that Shakespeare is an ordinary communicator. What makes Shakespeare (to name just one example) extraordinary is the way he exploited this ordinary aspect of communication so that a single line or phrase triggers the discovery of a whole array of implicatures.

9.3   Irony

Traditionally, irony is analysed in terms of meaning the opposite of what the sentence uttered literally means. Thus according to this analysis, the utterance in (5) (above) has two meanings – a literal meaning (*Barbara is always very tactful*) and a figurative meaning (*Barbara is always very tactless*). However, as have just seen, such an analysis fails to capture the indeterminacy of ironic utterances. Moreover, as we saw in chapter 6, there is a whole range of ironic utterances which simply cannot be analysed in these terms. It is difficult, for example, to see how the question in (15) could be interpreted as meaning the opposite of what it literally means, and yet, produced on a very rainy day, it would be interpreted as ironic.

(15)   Did you remember to water the garden?

As Wilson and Sperber (1989) have shown, quotations can be used ironically. Consider, for example, the utterance in (16) produced on a cold and wet day during an English spring.

(16)   Oh to be in England
       Now that April's there.

Is the speaker really expressing a desire not to be in England in April as the traditional analysis would suggest? Or is he making fun of romantic ideas about spring?

Irony is not always restricted to a couple of lines or a single utterance. In many cases it extends over a whole poem or story, so that it is difficult to identify a single utterance which gives rise to the ironic effect. Many of Dorothy Parker's stories and poems are ironic in this way. For example, in the the following excerpt Parker is ridiculing the behaviour of an elderly woman who continues to behave like a young woman. Clearly, it is the last two lines which contain the key to the irony. But their effect is to ensure that the reader understands the entire poem as ironic.

(17)   So let me have the rouge again,
       And comb my hair the curly way.
       The poor young men, the dear young men
       They'll all be here by noon today.
       .   .   .
       So bring my scarlet slippers, then,
       And fetch the powder puff to me.
       The dear young men, the poor young men –
       They think I'm only seventy.

       (Dorothy Parker, 'Ninon de Lenclos, on her
       Last Birthday')

It is difficult to see how such examples could be accommodated in the traditional account of irony.

In chapter 6 it was suggested that irony should be analysed in terms of the notion of *interpretive resemblance*, and more particularly on the notion of *echoic use*.[1] As we have just seen, every utterance is an interpretation of the thought that the speaker wishes to communicate. But a thought is a representation too, and as such it may be presented as an interpretation of another speaker's thought. We have already considered quite ordinary examples of utterances used to interpret someone else's speech or thought. Consider the dialogue in (18):

(18)   A: Did you see Nigel on Saturday?
       B: Yes. He is never going to speak to me again.

The second segment of B's reply has two possible interpretations. It might be a straightforward assertion of B's belief that Nigel will never speak to them again. Alternatively, it could be a report of what Nigel had said, or, in other words, an interpretive representation of what Nigel said. It will be recalled that Sperber and Wilson call an utterance which is understood in this second way *echoic*.

Suppose that that Nigel did actually produce the utterance in (19).

(19)   I am never going to speak to you again.

This is, of course, not fully identical to B's own utterance. Nonetheless the proposition it expresses is identical to the one expressed by B's utterance, and accordingly, it may be regarded as a completely *literal* interpretation of what Nigel said.

Now suppose that what Nigel said was (20).

(20)   Next time you come I shall pretend I don't know you.

In this case the proposition expressed by B's utterance is not identical to the proposition expressed by Nigel's utterance. However, we can still say that B's utterance is an interpretation of Nigel's utterance, albeit a less than literal one.

While the proposition expressed by B's utterance is not identical to the one expressed by Nigel's utterance, they do share certain properties. In particular, they share certain logical and contextual implications. For example, it is not difficult to think of a context in which Nigel's utterance in (20) contextually implies the proposition expressed by B's utterance. Nor is it difficult to think of a context in which the two utterances give rise to the same set of contextual implications. Obviously, the more shared properties, the greater the degree of interpretive resemblance.

Irony may involve literal resemblance. Recall Sperber and Wilson's example discussed in chapter 6:

(21) SHE: It's a lovely day for a picnic.
    (*They go for a picnic and it rains*)
    SHE: It's a lovely day for a picnic indeed.

However, it may also involve the loose kind of resemblance illustrated above. Notice too that an ironic utterance is not necessarily an interpretation of a thought which a speaker has actually expressed. It is frequently an interpretation of a thought which the speaker attributes to someone else. Thus, while Joseph Sedley may not have actually claimed that he was an invalid, there is plenty of evidence that this is what he believed. And Dorothy Parker's poem cited in (17) can be thought of as an interpretation of a whole block of attributed thoughts.

In fact, an ironic utterance is not necessarily an interpretation of a thought that can be attributed to any specific person. Suppose that you and I are looking at a shop window displaying what I believe to be some particularly ugly china ornaments. My utterance in (22) is not an interpretation of any particular person's thought, but rather an interpretation of the kind of thought that I believe some people might have.

(22) I simply must have one of those.

What is the point of producing an utterance which is an interpretive representation of another person's thought? In some cases the relevance of an echoic utterance simply lies in the information it gives about the content of the attributed thought. For example, the relevance of B's utterance in (18) lies in the information it gives about what Nigel had said. However, in other cases the relevance of an echoic utterance lies in the information it gives about the speaker's attitude towards the attributed thought. This attitude may be one of endorsement. Consider, for example, how a hearer would interpret the second speaker's utterance in (21) in a situation in which the sun did shine. Alternatively, an echoic utterance may convey an attitude of rejection. This is the attitude conveyed by the utterance in (21) as it was originally presented. And this, of course, is the attitude that characterizes ironic utterances.

By dissociating himself from the opinion echoed, the speaker indicates that he does not hold it himself. Indeed, it may be obvious in the circumstances that he believes the opposite of the opinion echoed. The speaker in (21), for example, will be understood to be communicating that she believes that it is not a lovely day for a picnic. But as we have seen, the speaker of an ironic utterance does not simply reject the opinion that his utterance echoes. He usually rejects it with scorn or makes fun of it. In other words, in the circumstances described the speaker of (21) might understood to be strongly communicating the assumptions in (23) and (24).

(23)   The speaker believes that it is not a lovely day for a picnic.
(24)   The speaker believes that it is ridiculous to think that it is a lovely day for a picnic.

However, the notion of ridicule is a very vague one, and it is very difficult to pin down exactly what impression or emotion the speaker is intending to convey. As we have seen, we can account for the communication of impressions and attitudes in much the same terms as the communication of standard implicatures. Speakers do not always intend to communicate a specific set of assumptions: sometimes the speaker's intentions are less determinate so the hearer is simply encouraged to think along certain lines without necessarily coming to any specific conclusion. Thus we could say that the speaker in (21) achieves a mixture of strong and weak communication. On the one hand she strongly communicates the assumptions in (23) and (24), while on the other he weakly implicates a range of contextual effects that can be derived from these assumptions. The effect is to give the hearer a great deal of responsibility for deciding just how ridiculous it is for someone to think it was a lovely day for a picnic.

In this example the speaker could be regarded as having said one thing and meant the opposite. However, this hardly captures the speaker's intentions. In contrast, if we regard the speaker's utterance as echoic, then we can account for his attitude of ridicule. More generally, by analysing irony in terms of echoic interpretive use we can account for all those cases of irony that fall outside the classical definition. I leave it to the reader to confirm that this is the case for the examples discussed earlier in this section and the examples given in Exercise 3 in chapter 6.

That the speaker of an echoic utterance is dissociating himself from the thought it echoes may be evident to the hearer on the basis of the context. However, in many cases the speaker will give the hearer some sort of indication that this is how the utterance should be understood. In spoken discourse an ironist may use his tone of voice, facial expression or accompanying gestures. However, these resources are clearly not available to a writer. In some cases a writer may rely upon the reader to recognize the absurdity of the thought or opinion echoed. For example, in the poem cited in (17) Parker assumes that we share her opinion that the behaviour she describes does not become a woman of 70, let alone a woman of 80 or more.

However, a writer may give the reader a clue as to the attitude she is expected to adopt. For example, in (3) (repeated below) Thackeray does not simply rely on our knowledge that invalids often have very poor appetites: he also chooses vocabulary which is apparently inappropriate in the circumstances. Consider in particular his use of the phrase *contented himself with* and the verb *manage*. One would normally *content oneself* with much less than a bottle of claret. And the verb *manage* suggests that Sedley is having difficulty in eating – something that is very hard to reconcile with the amount he actually consumed.

(3)   Being an invalid, Joseph Sedley contented himself with a bottle of claret besides his Madeira before dinner, and he managed a couple of plates full of strawberries and cream, and twenty four little rout cakes that were lying neglected in a plate near him. (Thackeray, *Vanity Fair*)

Some writers use the voice of one character in order to dissociate themselves from the thoughts of another. For example in *Sense and Sensibility* Jane Austen mocks the feelings of sensibility expressed by Marianne through the voice of Elinor. In the following dialogue Austen has Elinor echo part of Marianne's first utterance in order to ridicule her over-sentimental memories of Norland. Then she juxtaposes Elinor's realistic and unromantic description of Norland with Marianne's rapturous one.

(25)   'And how does dear, dear Norland look?' cried Marianne.
'Dear, dear Norland', said Elinor, 'probably looks as it always does at this time of year. The woods and walks thickly covered with dead leaves'.
'Oh!, cried Marianne, 'with what transporting sensations have I formerly seen them fall! How have I delighted, as I walked, to see them driven in showers about me by the wind! What feelings have they, the season, the air altogether inspired.'

Although in the examples we have discussed the speaker/writer may have indicated his attitude towards the opinion it echoes, he has not made his attitude explicit. Compare (21) with (26):

(26)   SHE: It's a lovely day for a picnic.
(*They go for a picnic and it rains*)
SHE: It is ridiculous to say that it is a lovely day for a picnic.

This would not traditionally be regarded as irony. And yet it communicates the same sort of attitude which, according to the above account, is associated with irony. What is it about the implicit expression of ridicule or contempt that gives rise to the poetic effects associated with irony?

As we shall see in section 9.4, decisions about what to express explicitly and what to leave implicit depend on the speaker's estimation of the hearer's contextual resources. A speaker will leave his attitude implicit only if he believes that the hearer has immediate access to a context in which it can be identified with less effort than would be needed to process an explicit statement. This means that a speaker who leaves his attitude implicit suggests that the hearer and speaker share assumptions about what, for example, is ridiculous or absurd. It goes without saying that the idea that it is a lovely day for a picnic is absurd, or that Joseph Sedley's claim to be an invalid is ridiculous. In each case the speaker/writer implicates a range of contextual assumptions needed to establish the absurdity of the idea or claim. But in each case he suggests that he and the hearer/reader are intimate enough for these assumptions to be accessible without being made explicit. In other words, by leaving his attitude implicit the speaker/writer of an ironic utterance conveys a suggestion of complicity.

Clearly, this entails a risk. A hearer who fails to recognize that the utterance is echoic in this way and that the speaker is dissociating himself from the thought echoed will be misled about the speaker's attitude to the proposition expressed and about his beliefs. Recall the example in (22) (repeated below) in which the speaker and hearer are looking at china ornaments in a shop window.

(22)   I simply must have one of those.

A hearer who is not particularly well acquainted with the speaker's tastes may not recognize the utterance as echoic, and may assume, mistakenly, that the speaker admires the ornament. On the other hand, if such a hearer does recognize the irony, the utterance will have the effect of increasing the degree of intimacy between them – the hearer will know, for example, that she can join in the joke by making fun of some other object in the window. It is this – the increase in intimacy – that makes the risk of misinterpretation worth taking.

Exercise 2

According to the *Princeton Encyclopedia of Poetry*, parody is the exaggerated imitation of a work of art (Preminger 1974). To what extent can the traditional definition of irony capture the links between irony and parody? Using examples, show how you might account for the similarities and differences between irony and parody in terms of the echoic account just outlined.

9.4 Style

Poetic Style

If this account of the effects of irony is correct, then we cannot view the speaker's choice of style – in particular, his decision to convey his attitude by an ironic utterance – independently of the message he wishes to convey. The decision to convey his attitude implicitly by means of an echoic utterance contributes to the interpretation of his utterance. On the other hand, in this account the notion of import or interpretation is not analysed in terms of a specific set of propositions that the speaker intended to communicate. It may include a whole range of propositions, no single one of which is specifically intended by the speaker. And the result is an effect on the relationship between speaker and hearer which could not have been achieved by a non-figurative utterance.

Our discussion of metaphor led to the same conclusion. A speaker who chooses to present a less than literal interpretation of his thoughts does so in the belief that this is the optimally relevant means of conveying those thoughts. In other words, poetic style is a consequence of the speaker's aim of producing an utterance consistent with the principle of relevance.

As we have seen, metaphorical and ironic utterances vary in their degree of creativity. The more creative the figure, the greater the responsibility the hearer has in the interpretation process. This does not mean, however, that a hearer or reader is generally given total responsibility so that the speaker/writer plays no role at all in the way the utterance is interpreted. For if this were so, then there would be no point in thinking that communication was taking place at all, at least not in the sense of *communication* that we have been developing here. In this sense, a speaker who engages in communication intends the hearer to recognize the intended content, context and contextual effects. A speaker could not engage in communication (in this sense) by producing an utterance which did not enable the hearer to recognize his intentions. There is a difference between creativity and gobbledegook. [2]

According to some theorists, the difference between poetry and gobbledegook resides not in the text itself, but in the way that the text is read. In other words, a poem is a poem because it is read as a poem. This means that if I write down just anything here, and ask you to interpret it as a poem, it is possible that you would do so. This is essentially the exercise which Fish (1980) performed with a group of students. He had left a list of names on the blackboard after a previous class, and then told his students that it was a religous poem that he wanted them to comment on. The fact that they were able to give an interpretation, claims Fish, shows that it is not what is in the text that counts, but the reading that is imposed on it.

However, as Pilkington (1989) says, if it was possible to create poems in this way, then 'fifteen minutes with a newspaper, scissors, paper and glue would be enough to prepare a complete manuscript to send off to Faber and Faber' (1989: 121). Moreover, Fish's conventionalist view does not explain the difference between the first and the final draft of a poem. What is the point of redrafting a poem, if what you write has no effect on the way it is interpreted? [3]

With a very creative metaphor such as the one in (14) (repeated below) different hearers with different imaginations and background knowledge will follow different routes in search of an interpretation, but it does not mean that the interpretation they recover is entirely imposed on the text.

(14)   'Tis not a year or two but show us a man,
       They are all but stomachs and we all but food;
       They eat us hungerly, and when they are full,
       They belch us.

Every hearer (or reader) is guided and encouraged by the text in the sense that it gives access to contextual assumptions which yield implicatures. What distinguishes this example from the more mundane examples of metaphor we have considered is that a creative hearer is encouraged to take a greater share of the responsibility in the interpretation process, so that the extra effort she invests is rewarded by a wide array of very weak implicatures, which she is encouraged to explore.

This means that a creative figure will succeed only to the extent that the hearer (or reader) is prepared to take this responsibility. By the same token, it means that a speaker/writer who communicates his thoughts by means of such an utterance is indicating that he assumes that the hearer/reader is prepared and, indeed, able to take this responsibility. As anyone who reads poetry will recognize, the interpretation of figurative utterances can entail a great deal of effort. But this does not mean that the poet's aim was to present a *puzzle* in interpretation. As Pilkington says, 'a poem does not deliberately set out to be obscure, to turn interpretation into a problem or issue' (1989: 132). If there is difficulty, then it is more likely that the poet has sacrificed what Seamus Heaney calls 'decency' – accessibility – to 'accuracy' – that is, accuracy in representing his feelings.[4] However, the result is what Sperber and Wilson have defined as a poetic effect, and the effort that the hearer expends is rewarded by a closer relationship with the poet.

Helping the Hearer

Talk of style normally occurs when a writer or speaker is perceived to have done something special, to have put a certain amount of time and effort into the formulation of his message. However, as we have seen, every serious speaker/writer aims to achieve adequate contextual effects for minimum processing effort, and this means that he must make some assumptions about the hearer's contextual resources and processing abilities. These assumptions will be reflected in the way in which he communicates his message. In other words, every speaker/writer who is aiming for optimal relevance must make a decision about the style of his communication.

In the first place, every speaker must make a decision about what to make explicit and what to leave implicit. Recall the sequence discussed in chapter 2, repeated here as (27). When this example was introduced it was assumed that you would be rather perplexed by it, since the first segment was unlikely to give you access to the contextual assumptions needed for the interpretation of the second.

(27) The river had been dry for a long time. Everyone attended the funeral.

If I had wanted to achieve optimal contextual effects, then I would have taken account of your contextual resources and made the necessary assumptions explicit, as in (28):

(28) When a river dries up a river spirit has died. When a river spirit dies there is a funeral. The river had been dry for some time. Everyone attended the funeral.

The difference between (27) and (28) does not lie in their contextual effects, but rather in the extent to which the speaker helps the hearer in obtaining those effects. Notice that while (28) might have been an appropriate utterance to produce for a Western hearer, it would have been inappropriate had the hearer been a Sissala speaker. For the first segment of (27) would have given such a hearer immediate access to the contextual assumptions required for the interpretation of the second, which means that the extra processing entailed by making these assumptions explicit would not have been rewarded by any contextual effect. In other words, (28) would have seemed unduly ponderous.

Exercise 3

1   Which of the following would be more appropriate in a casual conversation with your friends? Why?

   (a)   Simon and Jane have moved into their new house. Everyone is invited to the party.
   (b)   Simon and Jane have moved into their new house. When someone moves into a new house it is usual for them to hold a party. Everyone is invited.

2   Discuss the role of the segment in italic in the interpretation of the following text. Some readers might find Carver's style in this excerpt ponderous. Why?

> He [John Gardner] didn't look anywhere near what I imagined a writer should look like. The truth is, in those days he looked and dressed like a Presbyterian minister, or an FBI man. He always wore a black suit, a white shirt, and a tie. And he had a crewcut. (*Most of the young men of my age wore their hair in what was called a 'DA' style – a 'ducks ass' – the hair combed back along the sides of the head onto the nape and plastered down with hair oil or cream.*) (Raymond Carver, *Fires*)

Sequences such as the one in (28) and the ones in Exercise 3 above raise an interesting problem for a theory of utterance understanding. For they contain segments which do not yield adequate contextual effects in their own right, but whose relevance lies largely in the way they help the hearer in processing the surrounding text. Thus for example, in Exercise 3.2 the information in parentheses simply enables the hearer to appreciate more fully the contrast between Gardner and other young writers of the time. This suggests that the speaker cannot be aiming at optimal relevance in the first segment and then aiming at optimal relevance in the next. Rather it seems that he is trying to optimize relevance over the whole text.

   The sequences in (29) and (30) illustrate a related point.

(29)   Do you remember the man who bought your car? Well, he's doing a first year Philosophy course.

(30)   Do you see that building over there? Apparently, it is sinking about a foot a year.

The questions in these sequences are intended to function as reminders. However, they remind the hearer of information which is not optimally relevant in its own right, but which contributes to the relevance of a subsequent utterance by ensuring that certain contextual assumptions are accessible for its interpretation.

According to Hurford and Heasley (1983), an utterance is 'any stretch of talk, by one person, before and after which there is silence on the part of that person' (1983: 15). This definition raises a number of difficulties. Many readers will have had the experience of being subjected to long monologues and lectures delivered at speed. Does a whole lecture or one-sided conversation consist of a single utterance? Many readers will also have had the experience of having had another speaker interrupt them and complete their utterance. Is the result two utterances or one?

According to the relevance-theoretic framework we have adopted here, an utterance is an act of communicative behaviour which creates a presumption of optimal relevance. This means that it may be possible for two speakers to be engaged in producing a single utterance. It also means that a long monologue or lecture may consist of several utterances. At the same time, however, examples like the ones in (29) and (30) suggest that a speaker may optimize relevance over a whole text. The problem is, how do we characterize the initial segments of these sequences (or the segment in parentheses of Exercise 3.2? Elsewhere (Blakemore 1991) I have described such sequences in terms of one act of communication which is designed to help the hearer with the processing of another. But it is not clear in what sense the inital segments of (29) and (30) or the underlined segment of (b) can be regarded as an act of communication – at least not if an act of communication is defined in terms of something which creates optimal relevance.[5]

I do not wish to suggest here that an utterance may not yield contextual effects of its own and at the same time contribute to the relevance of a larger text. Consider the following excerpt and accompanying footnote from Sperber and Wilson (1986).

(31) There is a natural linkage between linguistic structure and pragmatic interpretation, and no need for any special pragmatic conventions or interpretation rules: the speaker merely adapts her utterance to the way the hearer is going to process it anyhow, given the existing structural and temporal constraints.[*]

[*] This is not to say, however, that no arbitary linkages between linguistic form and pragmatic interpretation exist . . .

The role of the footnote could be described in terms of the way it helps the hearer interpret the main text. In particular, it restricts the implicatures that the hearer may have otherwise derived from the main text. At the same time, one would not want to say that the claim that there *are* arbitrary linkages between linguistic form and pragmatic interpretation has no contextual effects of its own.[6]

A similar point is illustrated by the example of extended irony we considered in section 9.3 – the Dorothy Parker poem cited in (17). As we saw, there is no single line which could be said to contain the irony. The writer's attitude is communicated by the poem as a whole. At the same time, the poem can be divided into units each of which has its own contextual effects.

As we have seen, a speaker may produce an utterance in the expectation that it will achieve optimal relevance, but not have any specific expectations as to what contextual effects the hearer will derive. For example, in the dialogue below B's answer leaves the hearer free to derive any contextual effects she likes.

(32)   A: Have you read Anne's latest article?
       B: No.

In contrast, the indirect answer in (33) constrains the hearer's search for relevance. In particular, the hearer is directed towards a context which includes the assumption that Anne's article is written in French, and which allows her to derive the contextual implication that B has not read the article. She is also encouraged to derive some additional conclusions from the assumption that B does not read French. Thus although both responses communicate the same assumption – the assumption that B has not read the article, they communicate it in different ways. And the difference is a difference in the extent to which the hearer is constrained in her search for relevance. This can surely be regarded as another aspect of stylistic variation.

(33)   A: Have you read Anne's latest article?
       B: I don't read French.

In this example, the hearer is not so much constrained by the linguistic properties of the utterance as she is by the speaker's decision to force her to undertake extra processing in order to recover an interpretation consistent with the principle of relevance. In other words, the speaker is exploiting the hearer's assumption that the utterance is optimally relevant. However, we have also seen that a speaker may use the linguistic form of his utterance to guide the interpretation process. Consider, for example, the function of the discourse connectives *after all*, and *you see* as they are used in sequences like (34) and (35).

(34) I'm not going to the lecture today. You see, Nigel won't be there.

(35) I'm not going to the lecture today. After all, Nigel won't be there.

Or, recall the effect of focal stress in examples like those in (36) and (37).

(36) Jane borrowed the CAR.

(37) Jane BORROWED the car.

It will be recognized that styles vary according to the extent to which the speaker uses linguistically specified devices to constrain the hearer's choice of context, and according to the means they choose (lexical, syntactic or intonational). In each case, the speaker's decision is governed by his estimation of the hearer's processing abilities and contextual resources. In other words, it is a decision which arises out of the search for relevance.

Style is not an optional accessory worn like a tie or necklace. Every speaker must choose some form in which to communicate his message, and his decision is determined not by his aim to please the hearer's aesthetic sense, but by his aim to produce an optimally relevant utterance. Moreover, the speaker's decision will have an effect on the import of his utterance.

In this final section we have seen that *every* speaker must make some decision about what to make explicit and what to leave implicit, and that *every* speaker must make a decision about the extent to which he should use the linguistic form of his utterance to guide the interpretation process. In contrast with these mundane, everyday dimensions of style, the questions we considered earlier in the chapter about poetic style might seem more glamorous. After all, poetic style is not something that can be achieved by just anybody. I do not wish to deny that the effects achieved by poetic utterances are special. At the same time, to the extent that he is taken to be engaged in communication, a poet is just like any other communicator in that he will be taken to have created a presumption of optimal relevance, and the hearer/reader is entitled to expect that her processing effort will be rewarded by contextual effects. As we all know, reading poetry can be very difficult. Poetic utterances are distinguished from the more mundane cases of communication by the way that they encourage the hearer to take a greater share of the interpretation process, so that the extra effort she invests is rewarded by a wide array of very weak implicatures, which she is encouraged to explore.

The Romantics would have us believe that *all* language is metaphorical. However, it is clear that much of everyday communication does not attempt any degree of creativity at all. But ordinary utterances and poetic utterances share a fundamental property – they create a presumption of optimal relevance – and that hearers approach all utterances with this in mind. Moreover, as I have tried to show, to say that a phenomenon is ordinary and everyday is not necessarily to say that it is uninteresting.

Recommended Reading

Poetic Effects and Style

Sperber and Wilson 1986: 217–24.
Butler 1984: ch. 2, ch. 5 (sections 3 and 4).
Ray 1984: 1–6 (an introduction to these issues in literary theory).
Fish 1980.

Interpretive Resemblance

Sperber and Wilson 1986: 224–31

Irony

Sperber and Wilson 1986: 237–42
Grice 1978: 123–5; 1989: 53–4.

Metaphor

Sperber and Wilson 1985/6; 1986: 231–7.
Ortony 1979: 1–18 (for an introduction to the issues).
Davidson 1980.

The literature on metaphor is vast. Ortony (1979) contains a wide variety of papers, including a selection on metaphor and pragmatics.

Notes

1 It is interesting to compare the account that follows with Sperber and Wilson's earlier (1981) account which analyses irony in terms of *echoic mention*. Wilson and Sperber (1989) argue that this previous account was not only too restrictive, but also mistaken in its suggestion that the interpretation of non-literal utterances may involve entirely different representational and computational resources from those involved in the interpretation of literal utterances.

2 This is not to say that a hearer or reader is always free to derive contextual effects on her own initiative, using assumptions she herself has supplied on her own responsibility. But this lies outside communication, as we have defined it here.

3 For further discussion of this point see Pilkington (1989).

4 This distinction, which was made by Seamus Heaney at a public poetry reading in 1986, is cited by Pilkington (1989).

5 It would be interesting to consider parenthetical phenomena, for example, appositive relative clauses, from the point of view of this problem. It may be recognized that the same problem is raised by by analysis of performative utterances (see chapter 6).

6 If you are not sure what these contextual effects are, see sections 8.2 and 8.3.

References

Allan, K. 1986: *Linguistic Meaning*, vol. 1. London: Routledge & Kegan Paul.

Allwood, J., Andersson, L. G. and Dahl, O. 1977: *Logic in Linguistics*. Cambridge: Cambridge University Press.

Ariel, M. 1988: Referring and accessibility. *Journal of Linguistics*, 24, 65–87.

Ariel, M. 1990: *Accessing NP Antecedents*. London: Routledge.

Aristotle 1940: *Art of Poetry*, ed. W. Hamilton-Fyfe. Oxford: Oxford University Press.

Atlas, J. and Levinson, S. 1981: It-clefts, informativeness and logical form: radical pragmatics (revised standard version). In P. Cole (ed.), 1–57.

Austin, J. L. 1962: *How to do Things with Words*. Oxford: Clarendon.

Bach, K. and Harnish, R. 1979: *Linguistic Communication and Speech Acts*. Cambridge, Mass.: MIT Press.

Bar-Hillel, Y. (ed.) 1971: *Pragmatics of Natural Language*. Dordrecht: Reidel.

Bar-Lev, Z. and Palacas, A. 1980: Semantic command over pragmatic priority. *Lingua*, 51, 137–46.

Barnes, J. 1984: Evidentials in the Tuyuca verb. *International Journal of American Linguistics*, 50, 255–71.

Bauerle, R. et al. (eds) 1979: *Semantics from Different Points of View*. Berlin: Springer.

Bell, M. 1975: Questioning. *Philosophical Quarterly*, 25, 193–212.

Blakemore, D. 1987: *Semantic Constraints on Relevance*. Oxford: Blackwell.

Blakemore, D. 1988: The organization of discourse. In F. Newmeyer (ed.), vol. 4, 229–50.

Blakemore, D. 1989a: Linguistic form: the explicit and the implicit. In L. Hickey (ed.), 28–51.

Blakemore, D. 1989b: Denial and contrast: a relevance theoretic analysis of *but*. *Linguistics and Philosophy*, 12, 15–38.

Blakemore, D. 1991: Performatives and parentheticals. *Proceedings of the Aristotelian Society*, 91, 197–214.

Blass, R. 1985: Cohesion, Coherence and Relevance. University College London mimeo.

Blass, R. 1990: *Relevance Relations in Discourse*. Cambridge: Cambridge University Press.

Boden, M. 1977: *Artificial Intelligence and Natural Man*. Brighton: Harvester.

Bolinger, D. 1978: Yes–no questions are not alternative questions. In H. Hiz (ed.), 87–106.

Brown, G. and Yule, G. 1983: *Discourse Analysis*. Cambridge: Cambridge University Press.

Brown, P. and Levinson, S. 1978: Universals in language usage: politeness phenomena. In E. Goody (ed.), 56–311.

Brown, P. and Levinson, S. 1979: Social structure, groups and interaction. In K. Scherer and H. Giles (eds), 291–347.

Butler, C. 1984: *Interpretation, Deconstruction and Ideology*. Oxford: Oxford University Press.

Carlson, L. 1984: *'Well' in Dialogue Games*. Amsterdam: John Benjamins.

Carston, R. 1988a: Language and cognition. In F. Newmeyer (ed.) vol. 3, 38–68.

Carston, R. 1988b: Implicature, explicature and truth-theoretic sematics. In R. Kempson (ed.), 155–82.

Carston, R. 1990: Quantity maxims and generalised implicature. *UCL Working Papers in Linguistics*, 2, 1–31.

Chomsky, N. 1976: *Reflections on Language*. London: Fontana.

Chomsky, N. 1980: *Rules and Representations*. Oxford: Blackwell.

Chomsky, N. 1986: *Knowledge of Language: Its Nature, Origin and Use*. New York: Praeger.

Clark, B. 1989: A relevance-based approach to pseudo-imperatives. *UCL Working Papers in Linguistics*, 1, 53–74.

Clark, B. 1991: *Relevance Theory and the Semantics of Non-Declarative Sentences*. University College London Ph.D. dissertation.

Clark, H. 1977: Bridging. In P. Johnson-Laird and P. Wason (eds), 411–20.

Clark, H. and Marshall, C. 1981: Definite reference and mutual knowledge. In A. Joshi, B. Webber and I. Sag (eds), 10–63.

Cohen, L. J. 1971: Some remarks on Grice's views about the logical particles. In Y. Bar-Hillel (ed.), 51–68.

Cole, P. (ed.) 1978: *Syntax and Semantics*, vol. 9: *Pragmatics*. New York: Academic.

Cole, P. (ed.) 1981: *Radical Pragmatics*. New York: Academic.

Cole, P. and Morgan, J. (eds) 1975: *Syntax and Semantics*, vol 3: *Speech Acts*. New York: Academic.

Coleridge, S. T. 1906: *Biographia Literaria*, rev. edn, ed. George Watson. London: Dent.

Dancy, J., Moravczik, J. and Taylor, C. (eds) 1988: *Human Agency: Language, Duty and Value*. Stanford: Stanford University Press.

Dascal, M. and Katriel, T. 1977: Between semantics and pragmatics: two types of *but* – Hebrew 'aval' and 'ela'. *Theoretical Linguistics*, 4, 143–72.

Davidson, D. 1979: What metaphors mean. In S. Sacks (ed.), 29–46.

Davidson, D. and Harman, G. (eds) 1972: *Semantics of Natural Language*. Dordrecht: Reidel.

Davies, M. 1989: Tacit knowledge and subdoxastic states. In A. George (ed.), 131–52.

Derbyshire, D. C. 1979: *Hixkaryana*. Lingua Descriptive Series 1. Amsterdam: North-Holland.

Derrida, Jacques 1974: White mythology. *New Literary History*, 6 (1), 5–74.

Dijk, T. van 1977: *Text and Context*. London: Longman.

Donaldson, T. 1980: *Ngiyamba: The Language of the Wangaaybuwan*. Cambridge: Cambridge University Press.

Donnellan, K. 1966: Reference and descriptions. *Philosophical Review*, 75, 281–304. Reprinted in D. Steinberg and L. Jakobovits (eds), 100–14.

Derbyshire, D. C. 1979: *Hixkaryana*. Lingua Descriptive Series 1. Amsterdam: North-Holland.

Dretske, F. 1981: *Knowledge and the Flow of Information*. Oxford: Blackwell.

Fillmore, C. J. and Langendoen, D. T. (eds) 1971: *Studies in Linguistic Semantics*. New York: Holt Rinehart & Winston.

Fish, S. 1980: *Is There a Text in This Class?* Cambridge, Mass.: Harvard University Press.

Fodor, J. D. 1977: *Semantics: Theories of Meaning in Generative Grammar*. Brighton: Harvester.

Flew, A. (ed.) 1966: *Essays in Conceptual Analysis*. London: Macmillan.

Fodor, Jerry 1983: *The Modularity of Mind*. Cambridge, Mass.: MIT Press.

Frege, G. 1892: On sense and meaning, tr. M. Black. In P. Geach and M. Black (eds) (1985), 56–78.

Gazdar, G. 1979: *Pragmatics: Implicature, Presupposition and Logical Form*. New York: Academic.

Geach, P. and Black, M. 1985: *Translations from the Philosophical Writings of Gottlob Frege*. Oxford: Blackwell.

George, A. (ed.) 1989: *Reflections on Chomsky*. Oxford: Blackwell.

Gettier, E. L. 1963: Is justified true belief knowledge? *Analysis*, 23, 121–3.

Gleitmen, L. 1965: Co-ordinating conjunctions in English. *Language*, 51, 260–93.

Goody, E. (ed.) 1978: *Questions and Politeness: Strategies in Social Interaction*. Cambridge: Cambridge University Press.

Green, G. 1989: *Pragmatics and Natural Language Understanding*. Hillsdale, NJ: Lawrence Erlbaum.

Grice, H. P. 1957: Meaning. *Philosophical Review*, 66, 377–88. Reprinted in D. Steinberg and L. Jakobovits (eds), 53–9.

Grice, H. P. 1975: Logic and conversation. In P. Cole and J. Morgan (eds), 41–58.

Grice, H.P. 1978: Further notes on logic and conversation. In P. Cole (ed.), 121–8.

Grice, H. P. 1981: Presupposition and conversational implicature. In P. Cole (ed.), 183–98.

Grice, H. P. 1989: *Studies in the Way of Words*. Cambridge, Mass.: Harvard University Press.

Haegeman, L. 1991: *Introduction to Government and Binding Theory*. Oxford: Blackwell.

Halliday, M. A. K. and Hasan, R. 1976: *Cohesion in English*. London: Longman.

Hickey, L. (ed.) 1989: *The Pragmatics of Style*. London: Routledge.

Hiz, H. (ed.) 1978: *Questions*. Dordrecht: Reidel.

Hobbs, J. R. 1977: Coherence and interpretation in English texts. *Proceedings IJCAI*. Cambridge, Mass.

Hobbs, J. R. 1978: Why is Discourse Coherent? Technical Note 176. SRI Projects 5844, 7510, 7910.

Hobbs, J. R. 1979: Coherence and conference. *Cognitive Science*, 3, 67–90.

Hopper, P. (ed.) 1982: *Tense – Aspect: Between Semantics and Pragmatics*. Amsterdam: John Benjamins.

Horn, L. 1972: *On the Semantic Properties of the Logical Operators in English*. Indiana Linguistics Club.

Horn, L. 1983: Greek Grice. In *Papers from the 9th Regional Meeting of the Chicago Linguistics Society*, 203–14.

Huntley, M. 1984: The semantics of English imperatives. *Linguistics and Philosophy*, 7, 103–33.

Hurford, J. and Heasley, B. 1983: *Semantics: A Coursebook*. Cambridge: Cambridge University Press.

Itani-Kaufman, R. 1989: Japanese Particle *tte* Observed in Utterance Final Position: A Relevance Theoretic Approach. Paper presented at the Autumn Meeting of the Linguistics Association of Great Britain.

Johnson-Laird, P. and Wason, P. 1977: *Thinking: Readings in Cognitive Science.* Cambridge: Cambridge University Press.

Joshi, A., Webber, B. and Sag, I. (eds) 1981: *Elements of Discourse Understanding.* Cambridge: Cambridge University Press.

Karttunen, L. 1974: On Pragmatic and Semantic Meaning. Paper presented at the 11th Annual Philosophy Colloquium.

Karttunen, L. and Peters, S. 1975: Conventional implicature in Montague Grammar. *Proceedings of the Berkeley Linguistics Society,* 4, 266–78.

Katz, J. and Postal, P. 1964: *An Integrated Theory of Linguistic Descriptions.* Cambridge, Mass.: MIT Press.

Kempson, R. 1975: *Presupposition and the Delimitation of Semantics.* Cambridge: Cambridge University Press.

Kempson, R. 1977: *Semantic Theory.* Cambridge: Cambridge University Press.

Kempson, R. 1985: Pragmatics, anaphora and logical form. In D. Schiffrin (ed.), 1–10.

Kempson, R. (ed.) 1988: *Mental Representations: The Interface between Language and Reality.* Cambridge: Cambridge University Press.

Kempson, R. (forthcoming): *Language and Cognition: A Licensing Grammar.*

Kleiber, G. 1990: Marqueurs referentiels et processus interpretaifs: pour une approche 'plus semantique'. *Cahiers de Linguistique Française,* 11.

Lakoff, G. 1971: Presupposition and relative well-formedness. In D. Steinberg and L. Jakobovits (eds), 329–40.

Lakoff, G. and Johnson, M. 1980: *Metaphors We Live By.* Chicago: Chicago University Press.

Lakoff, R. 1971: Ifs, ands and buts about conjunction. In C. J. Fillmore and D. T. Langendoen (eds), 115–150.

Leech, G. N. 1983: *Principles of Pragmatics.* London: Longman.

Levinson, S. 1979: Pragmatics and social deixis. *Proceedings of the 5th Annual Meeting of the Berkeley Linguistics Society,* 206–23.

Levinson, S. 1983: *Pragmatics.* Cambridge: Cambridge University Press.

Levinson, S. 1987a: Minimization and conversational inference. In J. Verschueren and M. Bertucelli-Papi (eds), 61–129.

Levinson, S. 1987b: Pragmatics and the grammar of anaphora. *Journal of Linguistics,* 23, 379–434.

Levinson, S. 1987c: Generalised Conversational Implicature and the Semantics/ Pragmatics Interface. ms University of Cambridge.

Levinson, S. 1989: Review of Sperber and Wilson, *Relevance. Journal of Linguistics,* 25, 455–72.

Lewis, D. 1969: *Convention.* Cambridge, Mass.: Harvard University Press.

Lewis, D. 1972: General semantics. In D. Davidson and G. Harman (eds), 169–218.

Lewis, D. 1979: Scorekeeping in a language game. In R. Bauerle et al. (eds), 172–87.

Lightfoot, D. 1983: *The Language Lottery.* Cambridge, Mass.: MIT Press.

Lyons, J. 1977: *Semantics,* vol. 1. Cambridge: Cambridge University Press.

Montague, R. 1974: Pragmatics. In R. H. Thompson (ed.), *Formal Philosophy: Selected Papers.* New Haven: Yale University Press.

Newmeyer, F. 1983: *Grammatical Theory: Its Limits and Its Possibilities.* Chicago: University of Chicago Press.

Newmeyer, F. (ed.) 1988: *Linguistics: The Cambridge Survey,* vol. 1: *Linguistic Theory: Foundations;* vol. 3: *Language: Psychological and Biological Aspects:* vol. 4: *Language: The Socio-Cultural Context.* Cambridge: Cambridge University Press.

Oh, C. K. and Dineen, D. (eds) 1979: *Syntax and Semantics 11: Presupposition.* New

York: Academic.

Ortony, A. (ed.) 1979: *Metaphor and Thought*. Cambridge: Cambridge University Press.

Owen, M. L. 1983: *Apologies and Remedial Exchanges*. The Hague: Mouton.

Palmer, F. R. 1986: *Mood and Modality*. Cambridge: Cambridge University Press.

Pateman, T. 1986: Relevance, contextual effects and least effort. *Poetics Today*, 7, 745–54.

Pilkington, A. 1989: Poetic effects: a relevance perspective. *UCL Working Papers in Linguistics*, 1, 119–35.

Posner, R. 1980: Semantics and pragmatics of sentence connectives in natural languages. In J. Searle, F. Kiefer and M. Bierwisch (eds), 169–203.

Preminger, A. (ed.) 1974: *Princeton Encyclopedia of Poetry and Poetics*. London: Macmillan.

Prince, E. 1981: Towards a taxonomy of given–new information. In P. Cole (ed.), 223–56.

Ray, W. 1984: *Literary Meaning: From Phenomenology to Deconstruction*. Oxford: Blackwell.

Recanati, F. 1986: On defining communicative intentions. *Mind and Language*, vol 1, 213–42.

Recanati, F. 1987: *Meaning and Force: The Pragmatics of Performative Utterances*. Cambridge: Cambridge University Press.

Recanati, F. 1989: The pragmatics of what is said. *Mind and Language*, 4, 295–329.

Reinhart, T. 1983: *Anaphora and Semantic Interpretation*. London: Croom Helm.

Russell, B. 1919: *Introduction to Mathematical Philosophy*. London: George Allen & Unwin.

Sacks, H., Schegloff, E. A. and Jefferson, G. 1974: A simplest systematics for the organization of turn-taking in conversation. *Language*, 50, 696–735.

Sacks, Sheldon (ed.) 1979: *On Metaphor*. Chicago: University of Chicago Press.

Scherer, K. and Giles, H. (eds) 1979: *Social Markers in Speech*. Cambridge: Cambridge University Press.

Schiffer, S. 1972: *Meaning*. Oxford: Clarendon.

Schiffrin, D. (ed.) 1985a: *Meaning, Form and Use in Context*. Georgetown: Georgetown University Press.

Schiffrin, D. 1985b: Conversational coherence: the role of *well*. *Language*, 61, 640–67.

Schmerling, S. 1982: How imperatives are special and how they aren't. *Chicago Linguistics Society: Parasession on Non-Declaratives*.

Searle, J. 1969: *Speech Acts*. Cambridge: Cambridge University Press.

Searle, J. 1975: Indirect speech acts. In P. Cole and J. Morgan (eds), 59–82.

Searle, J. 1979: The classification of speech acts. In John Searle, *Expression and Meaning*, Cambridge: Cambridge University Press, 1–29.

Searle, J. 1989: How performatives work. *Linguistics and Philosophy*, 12, 535–58.

Searle, J., Kiefer, F., and Bierwisch M. (eds) 1980: *Speech Act Theory and Pragmatics*. Amsterdam: Reidel.

Shelley, P. B. 1820: A defence of poetry. In F. B. Brett-Smith (ed.), *The Four Ages of Poetry. etc.*, Oxford: Blackwell, 1923.

Slobin, D. and Aksu, A. 1982: Tense, aspect and modality in the use of the Turkish evidential. In P. Hopper (ed.), 185–200.

Smith, N. (ed.) 1982: *Mutual Knowledge*. London: Academic.

Sontag, S. 1987: On style. In S. Sontag, *Against Interpretation*. London: André Deutsch.

Sperber, D. and Wilson, D. 1981: Irony and the use-mention distinction. In P. Cole (ed.), 295–317.

Sperber, D. and Wilson, D. 1982: Mutual knowledge and relevance in theories of comprehension. In N. Smith (ed.), 61–131.

Sperber, D. and Wilson, D. 1985: Draft of *Relevance* (1986). University College London mimeo.

Sperber, D. and Wilson, D. 1985/6: Loose Talk. *Proceedings of the Aristotelian Society*, 86, 153–71.

Sperber, D. and Wilson, D. 1986: *Relevance: Communication and Cognition*. Oxford: Blackwell.

Sperber, D. and Wilson, D. 1987: Precis of *Relevance* (plus Open Peer Commentary and Authors' Response). *Behavioural and Brain Sciences*, 10, 697–754.

Stalnaker, R. 1972: Pragmatics. In D. Davidson and G. Harman (eds), 380–97.

Steinberg, D. and Jakobovits L. (eds) 1971: *Semantics: An Interdisciplinary Reader in Philosophy, Linguistics and Psychology*. Cambridge: Cambridge University Press.

Strawson, P. F. 1956: On referring. In Strawson (1971), 1–27.

Strawson, P. F. 1964: Intention and convention in speech acts. In Strawson (1971), 149–69.

Strawson, P. F. 1971: *Logico-Linguistic Papers*. London: Methuen.

Stubbs, Michael 1983: *Discourse Analysis: The Sociolinguistic Analysis of Natural Language*. Oxford: Blackwell.

Taylor, John R. 1989: Possessive genitives in English. *Linguistics*, 27, 663–86.

Travis, Charles (ed.) 1986: *Meaning and Interpretation*. Oxford: Blackwell.

Urmson, J. O. 1966: Parenthetical verbs. In A. Flew (ed.), 192–212.

Verschueren, J. and Bertucelli-Papi, N. (eds) 1987: *The Pragmatic Perspective*. Amsterdam: John Benjamins.

Werth, P. (ed.) 1981: *Conversation and Discourse*. London: Croom Helm.

Wilson, D. 1990: Pragmatics and Time. Paper delivered at the MIT Conference on Time in Language, April 1990.

Wilson, D. (forthcoming): Reference and Relevance. In B. Münsch and R. Posner (eds), *Proceedings of the International Semiotics Conference on Reference (Basle 1989)*.

Wilson, D. and Sperber, D. 1979: Ordered entailments: an alternative to presuppositional theories. In C. K. Oh and D. Dineen (eds).

Wilson, D. and Sperber, D. 1981: On Grice's theory of conversation. In P. Werth (ed.), 155–78.

Wilson, D. and Sperber, D. 1986: Inference and implicature. In C. Travis (ed.), 45–76.

Wilson, D. and Sperber, D. 1988: Mood and the analysis of non-declarative sentences. In J. Dancy, J. Moravczik and C. Taylor (eds), 229–324.

Wilson, D. and Sperber, D. 1989: On verbal irony. *UCL Working Papers in Linguistics*, 1, 96–118.

Wilson, D. and Sperber, D. 1990: Linguistic form and relevance. *UCL Working Papers in Linguistics*, 2, 95–112.

Index

Note: As this book is grounded in Sperber and Wilson's Relevance Theory I have referred to them (either directly or indirectly) on virtually every page. Accordingly, in this index I have restricted references to Sperber and Wilson to the Recommended Reading lists where the reader is directed to the appropriate sources.